2002 Supplement
DISPUTE RESOLUTION

ASPEN PUBLISHERS, INC.
Legal Education Division

EDITORIAL ADVISORS

Erwin Chemerinsky
Sydney M. Irmas Professor of Public Interest Law, Legal Ethics, and Political Science
University of Southern California

Richard A. Epstein
James Parker Hall Distinguished Service Professor of Law
University of Chicago

Ronald J. Gilson
Charles J. Meyers Professor of Law and Business
Stanford University
Marc and Eva Stern Professor of Law and Business
Columbia University

James E. Krier
Earl Warren DeLano Professor of Law
University of Michigan

Richard K. Neumann, Jr.
Professor of Law
Hofstra University School of Law

Kent D. Syverud
Dean and Garner Anthony Professor
Vanderbilt University Law School

Elizabeth Warren
Leo Gottlieb Professor of Law
Harvard University School of Law

EMERITUS ADVISORS

E. Allan Farnsworth
Alfred McCormack Professor of Law
Columbia University

Geoffrey C. Hazard, Jr.
Trustee Professor of Law
University of Pennsylvania

Bernard Wolfman
Fessenden Professor of Law
Harvard University

DISPUTE RESOLUTION

Negotiation, Mediation, and Other Processes

Third Edition

Stephen B. Goldberg
Professor of Law
Northwestern University

Frank E.A. Sander
Bussey Professor of Law
Harvard University

Nancy H. Rogers
Dean and Moritz Chair in Alternative Dispute Resolution
Ohio State University, Moritz College of Law

2002 Supplement

Prepared by:
Sarah Rudolph Cole
Nancy H. Rogers
Frank E.A. Sander

ASPEN LAW & BUSINESS
A Division of Aspen Publishers, Inc.
New York   Gaithersburg

Copyright © 2002 by Stephen B. Goldberg, Frank E.A. Sander, Nancy H. Rogers, and Sarah Rudolph Cole

All rights reserved. No part of this publication may be reproduced or transmitted in any form or by any means, electronic or mechanical, including photocopy, recording, or any information storage and retrieval system, without permission in writing from the publisher. Requests for permission to make copies of any part of this publication should be mailed to:

Permissions
Aspen Law & Business
1185 Avenue of the Americas
New York, NY 10036

Printed in the United States of America

1 2 3 4 5 6 7 8 9 0

ISBN 0-7355-2880-2

Library of Congress Cataloging-in-Publication Data

Goldberg, Stephen B.
    Dispute resolution : negotiation, mediation, and other processes / Stephen B. Goldberg, Frank E.A. Sander, Nancy H. Rogers — 3rd ed.
    p.   cm.
    Includes bibliographical references and index.
    ISBN 0-7355-0019-3 (casebound)
    ISBN 0-7355-2880-2 (supplement)
    1. Dispute resolution (Law)—United States.   I. Sander, Frank E. A.   II. Rogers, Nancy H.   III. Title
KF9084.G55   1999
347.73'9 — dc21   99-28905
                                                                                        CIP

About Aspen Law & Business Legal Education Division

With a dedication to preserving and strengthening the long-standing tradition of publishing excellence in legal education, Aspen Law & Business continues to provide the highest quality teaching and learning resources for today's law school community. Careful development, meticulous editing, and an unmatched responsiveness to the evolving needs of today's discerning educators combine in the creation of our outstanding casebooks, coursebooks, textbooks, and study aids.

ASPEN LAW & BUSINESS
A Division of Aspen Publishers, Inc.
A Wolters Kluwer Company
www.aspenpublishers.com

Contents

Table of Cases   *xi*
Preface   *xiii*
Acknowledgments   *xv*

CHAPTER 1. DISPUTING PROCEDURES   1

    References   1

CHAPTER 2. NEGOTIATION   3

    Note on empathy and assertiveness and difficult conversations   3
    Additional reference on negotiating power   3
    Note on Question 2.12   4
    Note on Model Rule 4.1   4
    Exercise 2.10: The DONS Negotiation   5

CHAPTER 3. MEDIATION   7

    Note on mediator quality control   7
    ABA 2000 Rule 2.4   7
    References   9

CHAPTER 4. ARBITRATION   11

C. Mandatory Arbitration of Statutorily-Based Employment Disputes
    Post-*Gilmer* Issues   11

D.	EEOC's Continuing Role in Discrimination Cases		11
	EEOC v. Waffle House, Inc.		12
E.	Fairness in Arbitral Procedure: Who Should Pay Arbitrator's Fees?		18
	Question 4.11		20
F.	Continuing Role of State Law in Arbitration		20
	1.	Preemption	21
		Question 4.12	23
		Question 4.13	23
		Question 4.14	23
		Question 4.15	24
		Question 4.16	24
		Question 4.17	26
	2.	The Revised Uniform Arbitration Act	27
		Question 4.18	28
		Question 4.19	28
		Question 4.20	30
		Question 4.21	30
		Question 4.22	31
G.	Arbitration Ethics		31
	Question 4.23		32
	Question 4.24		33
	References		33

CHAPTER 5. COMBINING AND APPLYING THE BASIC PROCESSES 35

C.	Recommending a Process for a Case		35
	Additional reference on process selection		35
D.	Representing a Client in Dispute Resolution		35
	1.	Premediation	35
		Siemer, Perspectives of Advocates and Clients on Court-Sponsored ADR	35
	6.	Ethical Issues	38
		Note on ethical issues regarding lawyer representing parties in mediation	38
E.	Making the Decision to Settle: Decision Analysis		38
	Some Questions About Decision Analysis		38
F.	Dispute Systems Design		40
	Two Current Applications of Dispute Systems Design		40
	E-ADR		40

Contents

Question 5.27A	40
Streams of Cases	41
Question 5.27B	42
Question 5.27C	42
References	43

CHAPTER 6. COURTS AND ADR — 45

Note on mediator reporting — 45

CHAPTER 7. CONFIDENTIALITY — 47

Accommodating the Interests of Justice: Predictability Versus Fine Tuning	47
Olam v. Congress Mortgage Co.	47
Note on "Qualified" v. "Categorical" Privilege	51
Conflict of Laws	53
Question 7.10.1	53
Question 7.10.2	54
Question 7.10.3	54
Question 7.10.4	54
Question 7.10.5	54

CHAPTER 8. FAMILY DISPUTES — 55

Note on right to representation in family mediation — 55

CHAPTER 9. PUBLIC DISPUTES — 57

Additional reference on consensus-building — 57

CHAPTER 10. INTERNATIONAL DISPUTES — 59

Additional reference on international negotiation — 59

Contents

CHAPTER 11. THE FUTURE OF ADR   **61**

     Note on collaborative lawyering   61

APPENDIX H.   **REVISED UNIFORM ARBITRATION ACT (2000)**   **63**

APPENDIX I.   **ABA MODEL STANDARDS OF PRACTICE FOR FAMILY AND DIVORCE MEDIATION (2001)**   **83**

APPENDIX J.   **UNIFORM MEDIATION ACT (2002)**   **93**

Table of Cases

Principal cases are in italic type.

Armendariz v. Foundation Health Psychcare Services, Inc., 18
Bowen v. Amoco Pipeline Co., 30
Bradford v. Rockwell Semiconductor Systems, 18
Circuit City v. Adams, 21
Doctor's Associates v. Cassarotto, 21
Duffield v. Robertson Stephens & Co., 27
EEOC v. Waffle House, Inc., 12
Green Tree Financial Corp.-Alabama v. Randolph, 18
In re Knepp, 23
Lapine Tech Corp. v. Kyocera Corp., 30
Maciejewski v. Alpha Systems Lab, Inc., 18
Olam v. Congress Mortgage Co., 47
Powertel, Inc. v. Bexley, 23
Rosenberg v. Merrill Lynch, 18
Southland Corp. v. Keating, 21
Volt Information Sciences, Inc. v. Leland Stanford University, 28
Zumpano v. Omnipoint Communications, 18

Preface

Although it has been scarcely three years since the publication of the Third Edition, there have been a number of significant developments in the field that we wish to reflect. Foremost among these is the promulgation of the Uniform Mediation Act and the Revised Uniform Arbitration Act. Another evolving field is the validity of contractual arbitration, particularly cases involving claims under various protective statutes such as Title VII. And there continues to be a lively debate concerning the ethical issues raised by various ADR procedures.

These and other issues will be reflected more fully in the forthcoming Fourth Edition, which we hope to publish next year.

S.R.C.
N.H.R.
F.E.A.S.

April 2002

Acknowledgments

The authors gratefully acknowledge the permissions granted to reproduce the following materials.

AMERICAN BAR ASSOCIATION (2001). Proposed changes in Model Rules of Professional Conduct 2.4 and 1.12. Reprinted by permission.

DONS Negotiation (2000). © by President and Fellows of Harvard University. Reprinted by permission of the Clearinghouse at the Program on Negotiation.

Revised Uniform Arbitration Act (2000). © by National Conference of Commissioners of Uniform State Laws. Reprinted by permission.

SIEMER, Dianne (2001). Note on Attitude of Litigators Towards Mediation. Reprinted by permission.

SHAW, Margaret (2001). "Streams of Cases." Reprinted by permission.

Uniform Mediation Act (2001). © by National Conference of Commissioners of Uniform State Laws. Reprinted by permission.

2002 Supplement
DISPUTE RESOLUTION

1
DISPUTING PROCEDURES

Page 13. **Add the following References:**

BRUNET, Edward, and Charles B. CRAVER (2001) *Alternative Dispute Resolution: The Advocate's Perspective* (2d ed). Matthew Bender/LEXIS NEXIS.

STONE, Katherine V.W. (2000) *Private Justice: The Law of Alternative Dispute Resolution.* New York: Foundation Press.

WARE, Stephen J. (2001) *Alternative Dispute Resolution.* St. Paul: West.

2
NEGOTIATION

Page 64. **Read the following in connection with your study of the piece by Mnookin, Peppet, and Tulumello on the tension between empathy and assertiveness:**

The tension described at pp. 64-67, along with the tension between creating and claiming (cf. casebook pp. 51-62) and the tension between principal and agent (cf. casebook pp. 74-80), are the primary focus of the book, *Beyond Winning—Negotiating to Create Value in Deals and Disputes* (Cambridge: Harvard Univ. Press 2000) by these same three authors. The book focuses particularly on the role of lawyers in negotiation and the opportunities they present for problem solving and value creation.

Managing the tension between empathy and assertiveness is one aspect of the emotional issues that arise in negotiation. Another is posed by the challenge of handling a "difficult negotiation"—that is, a negotiation that is fraught with intense feelings on both sides, such as firing an ineffective but angry employee or saying no to a troubled, disorganized colleague who keeps asking you at 5 P.M. to help her complete her assigned work. This topic is addressed in an important new book, *Difficult Conversations*, by Douglas Stone, Bruce Patton, and Sheila Heen (New York: Viking 1999). The key, according to the authors, is to sort out three different conversations: (1) The "what happened?" conversation, which seeks to separate how each side sees the situation, distinguishing between *impact* on the listener ("you made me very angry") and the *intent* of the speaker; (2) the "feelings" conversation, which explores how each side feels about the matter being discussed; and (3) the "identity" conversation, which attempts to relate the experienced feelings to the participants' self-perception or identity.

Page 67. **For further elaboration of negotiating power, see Robert S. Adler and Elliot M. Silverstein (2000) " WhenDavid Meets Goliath: Dealing with Power Differentials in Negotiation."** *5 Harv. Neg. L. Rev. 1.*

Page 80. **In connection with Question 2.12, consider Deborah M. Kolb and Judith Williams (2000)** *The Shadow Negotiation: How Women Can Master the Hidden Agendas That Determine Bargaining Success* **New York: Simon and Schuster.**

On the basis of extensive interviews with women negotiators, the authors point out that often the primary negotiation across the table is significantly affected by a parallel "shadow" negotiation in which the negotiator comes to grips with her self-concept and her image of her negotiation strengths—or weaknesses. In order to have an effective across-the-table negotiation style, each negotiator must first skillfully manage this "shadow" negotiation. This entails a mastery of the issues in the case. But equally important is the development of a confident, self-assured persona.

Page 88. **In connection with Rule 4.1, consider the following:**

Despite occasional suggestions that Rule 4.1 is too minimalist, see, for example, James Alfini (1999) "Settlement Ethics and Lawyering in ADR Proceedings: A Proposal to Revise Rule 4.1," 19 *N. Ill. U. L. Rev.* 255, ABA 2000, the American Bar Association's review of the Model Rules of Professional Conduct, proposed no change in the rule itself. Rather it suggested a beefing up of the Commentary by (1) adding the word "ordinarily" in the third sentence under Statements of Fact ("Estimates of price or value placed on the subject of a transaction and a party's intention as to an acceptable settlement of a claim are ordinarily in this category...."); (2) expanding the third section of the Commentary to deal with "Crime or Fraud by Client"; and (3) adding cross references to Rules 1.2(d) and 8.4.

Suppose you were in general agreement with Professor Alfini that Rule 4.1 represents too much of a lowest ethical common denominator, how would you change the Rule? By adopting either of the following changes or some other formulation?

1. Delete the word "material" in 4.1(a);
2. Substitute for Rule 4.1 the following:

The lawyer must act honestly and in good faith in dealing with others.

For an altogether different approach, focusing not on deception and disclosure, but rather on the ethics of human interaction, see Jonathan R. Cohen (2001) "When People Are the Means: Negotiating with Respect," 14 *Geo. J. Legal Ethics* 739.

Chapter 2. Negotiation — Page 119

Page 119. Add the following new exercise:

EXERCISE 2.10: THE DONS NEGOTIATION*

General Instructions

The year is 2021 and the AIDS virus has been completely obliterated. Researchers at The John Hopkins University discovered a vaccine as well as a serum which cures the disease in mid-course. All children are now vaccinated for the disease shortly after birth. There has not been a case of AIDS reported in the United States since the serum was developed 18 years ago.

Five years ago, however, scientists discovered a new lethal virus, Dysfunction of the Nervous Systems, DONS. The disease can *only* be transmitted through either vaginal or anal intercourse. Unlike AIDS, it cannot be transmitted through blood transfusions. All persons who have contracted DONS have died from it within a range of four to six years. DONS can be detected in the bloodstream of the individual one to four months after entering the body, and there are highly accurate home testing kits. Thus far, there is no cure for DONS, and the only preventive measures available are abstention from sexual activity or the use of condoms.

On November 1, 2019, Chris Wilson engaged in unprotected sexual intercourse with her boyfriend of six months and contracted the DONS virus. On March 16, 2020, Chris tested positive for the virus. Upset and disillusioned, she denied that she had the disease for a period of several months.

Chris attended a social function in early June, however, where she met Pat Stevens. The two eventually became involved in a relationship and on August 2, 2020, they had sexual intercourse for the first time while staying at Chris's ranch in Montana. It was the first time in four and one-half years that Pat had engaged in intercourse.

Chris felt that Pat was a great support for her. She was able to tell Pat about the depression she felt over her youngest child Annie, who has leukemia. She told Pat that she was worried that she would not be able to meet the expenses of Annie's

---

*This case was created for the Harvard Negotiation Research Project by Nevan Elam and was revised by Whitney Fox. It was further revised by Bob Bordone & Jonathan Cohen of the Harvard Negotiation Research Project. Copies are available at a reasonable cost from the Program on Negotiation Clearinghouse, Pound Hall 500, Harvard Law School, Cambridge, MA 02138. Tel.: (617) 495-1684. This case may not be reproduced, revised, or translated in whole or part by any means without written permission from the Director of the Clearinghouse. Please help to preserve its usefulness by keeping it confidential. The fees charged for the use of Clearinghouse materials help to subsidize their distribution. Copyright © 1992, 1999 by the President and Fellows of Harvard College. All rights reserved.

treatment since the insurance policy had reached its maximum, and the cost of her treatment was approximately $200,000 per year. She told Pat that it had taken her five years to save $600,000, which she had set aside for Annie's expenses. Pat thought that Chris's deep depression was simply related to the cancer-stricken child, and he tried to be as supportive as possible.

The relationship lasted for four months, during which the two had numerous sexual relations without using condoms. Chris, still in denial about contracting the virus, did not care that she may have been infecting her new boyfriend with the deadly DONS disease. Later she didn't disclose it because it seemed the damage was probably done in all events. The relationship deteriorated, and on September 13, 2020, the two stopped dating. Their last sexual encounter was on September 2, 2020.

On January 2, 2021, Pat received a letter from Chris confessing that she had the DONS virus. In the letter, Chris told Pat that she had known she had the disease before their relationship, but that she was unable to tell Pat while they were dating. In the letter, Chris suggested that Pat be tested for DONS and expressed the hope that he would test negative. The next day Pat purchased a home testing kit but unfortunately tested positive for the virus. Pat spent the next month in a troubled emotional state, and on February 9, 2021, he wrote to Chris and told her that he planned to sue her for the cost of treatment and other damages. Chris responded on February 20, 2021, stating that the lawsuit would not be necessary. She suggested that their lawyers negotiate an agreeable settlement.

(Confidential information for both parties is contained in the Teacher's Manual.)

3
MEDIATION

Page 206. Insert before Questions:

Another indirect form of mediator quality control comes about through guidelines formulated for Provider Organizations. See Margaret L. Shaw and Elizabeth Plapinger (2001) "Ethical Guidelines—ADR Provider Organizations Should Increase Transparency, Disclosure" *Dis. Res. Mag.* 14 (Spring). See pp.31-32 (in this supplement) for a discussion of the applicability of these guidelines to arbitrators.

Page 218. Insert before Question:

ABA 2000 proposed the following new Rule:

RULE 2.4: LAWYER SERVING AS THIRD-PARTY NEUTRAL

(a) A lawyer serves as a third-party neutral when the lawyer assists two or more persons who are not clients of the lawyer to reach a resolution of a dispute or other matter that has arisen between them. Service as a third-party neutral may include service as an arbitrator, a mediator or in such other capacity as will enable the lawyer to assist the parties to resolve the matter.

(b) A lawyer serving as a third-party neutral shall inform unrepresented parties that the lawyer is not representing them. When the lawyer knows or reasonably should know that a party does not understand the lawyer's role in the matter, the lawyer shall explain the difference between the lawyer's role as a third-party neutral and a lawyer's role as one who represents a client.

Commentary

[1] Alternative dispute resolution has become a substantial part of the civil justice system. Aside from representing clients in dispute resolution processes, lawyers often serve as third-party neutrals. A third-party neutral is a person, such

as a mediator, arbitrator, conciliator or evaluator, who assists the parties, represented or unrepresented, in the resolution of a dispute or in the arrangement of a transaction. Whether a third-party neutral serves primarily as a facilitator, evaluator or decisionmaker depends on the particular process that is either selected by the parties or mandated by a court.

[2] The role of a third-party neutral is not unique to lawyers, although, in some court-connected contexts, only lawyers are allowed to serve in this role or to handle certain types of cases. In performing this role, the lawyer may be subject to court rules or other law that apply either to third-party neutrals generally or to lawyers serving as third-party neutrals. Lawyer-neutrals may also be subject to various codes of ethics, such as the Code of Ethics for Arbitration in Commercial Disputes prepared by a joint committee of the American Bar Association and the American Arbitration Association or the Model Standards of Conduct for Mediators jointly prepared by the American Bar Association, the American Arbitration Association and the Society of Professionals in Dispute Resolution.

[3] Unlike nonlawyers who serve as third-party neutrals, lawyers serving in this role may experience unique problems as a result of differences between the role of a third-party neutral and a lawyer's service as a client representative. The potential for confusion is significant when the parties are unrepresented in the process. Thus, paragraph (b) requires a lawyer-neutral to inform unrepresented parties that the lawyer is not representing them. For some parties, particularly parties who frequently use dispute-resolution processes, this information will be sufficient. For others, particularly those who are using the process for the first time, more information will be required. Where appropriate, the lawyer should inform unrepresented parties of the important differences between the lawyer's role as third-party neutral and a lawyer's role as a client representative, including the inapplicability of the attorney-client evidentiary privilege. The extent of disclosure required under this paragraph will depend on the particular parties involved and the subject matter of the proceeding, as well as the particular features of the dispute-resolution process selected.

[4] A lawyer who serves as a third-party neutral subsequently may be asked to serve as a lawyer representing a client in the same matter. The conflicts of interest that arise for both the individual lawyer and the lawyer's law firm are addressed in Rule 1.12. . . .

In addition, as indicated in the Commentary [4], it expanded Rule 1.12 dealing with conflicts of interest rules for former judges or arbitrators to extend also to mediators "and other third-party neutrals."

Chapter 3. Mediation

RULE 1.12: FORMER JUDGE ~~OR~~, ARBITRATOR, MEDIATOR OR OTHER THIRD-PARTY NEUTRAL

(a) Except as stated in paragraph (d), a lawyer shall not represent anyone in connection with a matter in which the lawyer participated personally and substantially as a judge or other adjudicative officer, ~~arbitrator~~ or law clerk to such a person <u>or as an arbitrator, mediator or other third-party neutral</u>, unless all parties to the proceeding <u>give informed</u> consent ~~after consultation~~, <u>confirmed in writing</u>.

(b) A lawyer shall not negotiate for employment with any person who is involved as a party or as lawyer for a party in a matter in which the lawyer is participating personally and substantially as a judge or other adjudicative officer or <u>as an</u> arbitrator, <u>mediator or other third-party neutral</u>. A lawyer serving as a law clerk to a judge, <u>or</u> other adjudicative officer ~~or arbitrator~~ may negotiate for employment with a party or lawyer involved in a matter in which the clerk is participating personally and substantially, but only after the lawyer has notified the judge, <u>or</u> other adjudicative officer ~~or arbitrator~~.

(c) If a lawyer is disqualified by paragraph (a), no lawyer in a firm with which that lawyer is associated may knowingly undertake or continue representation in the matter unless:

(1) the disqualified lawyer is <u>timely</u> screened from any participation in the matter and is apportioned no part of the fee therefrom; and

(2) written notice is promptly given to the <u>parties and any</u> appropriate tribunal to enable ~~it~~ <u>them</u> to ascertain compliance with the provisions of this rule.

(d) An arbitrator selected as a partisan of a party in a multimember arbitration panel is not prohibited from subsequently representing that party.

Carefully compare the CPR Georgetown Draft Rule 4.5.4 (p. 217) with the ABA 2000 proposals. What are the critical differences?

Page 225. Add the following References:

ALFINI, James J., Sharon B. PRESS, Jean R. STERNLIGHT, and Joseph B. STULBERG (2001) *Mediation Theory and Practice.* Matthew Bender/LEXIS.
CLOKE, Kenneth (2000) *Mediating Dangerously.* San Francisco: Jossey-Bass.
KOVACH, Kimberlee (2000) *Mediation—Principles and Practice.* St. Paul: West.
MENKEL-MEADOW, Carrie, ed. (2000) *Mediation—Theory, Policy and Practice.* Burlington, Vt.: Ashgate.

4
ARBITRATION

C. MANDATORY ARBITRATION OF STATUTORILY-BASED EMPLOYMENT DISPUTES

Page 250. **Add the following after the last line of text on the page:**

In addition to the three basic post-*Gilmer* issues, three new issues have arisen since *Gilmer* was decided:

- The impact of arbitration agreements on the EEOC's continuing role in employment discrimination cases;
- How the allocation of arbitrator's fees affects the fairness of the arbitration procedure; and
- The impact of proposed state and federal legislation on arbitration.

Each of these issues will be discussed seriatim following the discussion of the three basic issues on pp. 251-269.

Page 269. **Add the following material following the Questions:**

D. THE EEOC'S CONTINUING ROLE IN EMPLOYMENT DISCRIMINATION CASES

One of the questions remaining after *Gilmer* was what impact the existence of an arbitration agreement would have on the EEOC's ability to enforce federal antidiscrimination laws. The *Gilmer* Court acknowledged concern about the effect of its decision on the EEOC's efforts to eradicate workplace discrimination, but concluded that its decision would have a minimal impact on the EEOC for two reasons. First, the EEOC would continue to play a role in discrimination cases because arbitration agreements do not preclude an employee from filing a claim with the EEOC. Second, the existence of an arbitration agreement would have no effect on the EEOC's ability to seek class-wide and injunctive relief on behalf of claimants. Unfortunately, the *Gilmer* decision did not address whether the existence of an arbitration agreement would preclude the EEOC from pursuing monetary relief on behalf of the claimant.

The Supreme Court addressed the issue over ten years later in the case that follows.

EEOC v. WAFFLE HOUSE, INC.
122 S. Ct. 754 (2002)

STEVENS, JUSTICE, delivered the opinion of the Court.

The question presented is whether an agreement between an employer and an employee to arbitrate employment-related disputes bars the Equal Employment Opportunity Commission (EEOC) from pursuing victim-specific judicial relief, such as backpay, reinstatement, and damages, in an enforcement action alleging that the employer has violated Title I of the Americans with Disabilities Act of 1990 (ADA).

[Eric Baker agreed to arbitrate any dispute arising out of his employment at Waffle House. While at work, Baker suffered a seizure. Soon after he was discharged. Instead of filing a claim in arbitration, Baker filed with the EEOC. The EEOC decided to pursue his case, including a claim for victim-specific relief. The Fourth Circuit rejected the EEOC's claim, authorizing the EEOC to pursue only injunctive or equitable relief on behalf of an employee who had signed an arbitration agreement.]

IV.

The Court of Appeals based its decision on its evaluation of the "competing policies" implemented by the ADA and the FAA, rather than on any language in the text of either the statutes or the arbitration agreement between Baker and respondent. It recognized that the EEOC never agreed to arbitrate its statutory claim and that the EEOC has "independent statutory authority" to vindicate the public interest, but opined that permitting the EEOC to prosecute Baker's claim in court "would significantly trample" the strong federal policy favoring arbitration because Baker had agreed to submit his claim to arbitration. To effectuate this policy, the court distinguished between injunctive and victim-specific relief, and held that the EEOC is barred from obtaining the latter because any public interest served when the EEOC pursues "make whole" relief is outweighed by the policy goals favoring arbitration. Only when the EEOC seeks broad injunctive relief, in the Court of Appeals' view, does the public interest overcome the goals underpinning the FAA.

[The Court of Appeals] simply sought to balance the policy goals of the FAA against the clear language of Title VII and the agreement. While this may be a more coherent approach, it is inconsistent with our recent arbitration cases. The FAA directs courts to place arbitration agreements on equal footing with other contracts, but it "does not require parties to arbitrate when they have not agreed to do so." ... No one asserts that the EEOC is a party to the contract, or that it agreed to arbitrate its claims. It goes without saying that a contract cannot bind a nonparty. Accordingly, the proarbitration policy goals of the FAA do not require the agency to relinquish its statutory authority if it has not agreed to do so.

Even if the policy goals underlying the FAA did necessitate some limit on the EEOC's statutory authority, the line drawn by the Court of Appeals between injunctive and victim-specific relief creates an uncomfortable fit with its avowed purpose of preserving the EEOC's public function while favoring arbitration. For that purpose, the category of victim-specific relief is both overinclusive and underinclusive. For example, it is overinclusive because while punitive damages benefit the individual employee, they also serve an obvious public function in deterring future violations. Punitive damages may often have a greater impact on the behavior of other employers than the threat of an injunction, yet the EEOC is precluded from seeking this form of relief under the Court of Appeals' compromise scheme. And, it is underinclusive because injunctive relief, although seemingly not "victim-specific," can be seen as more closely tied to the employees' injury than to any public interest.

The compromise solution reached by the Court of Appeals turns what is effectively a forum selection clause into a waiver of a nonparty's statutory remedies. But if the federal policy favoring arbitration trumps the plain language of Title VII and the contract, the EEOC should be barred from pursuing any claim outside the arbitral forum. If not, then the statutory language is clear; the EEOC has the authority to pursue victim-specific relief regardless of the forum that the employer and employee have chosen to resolve their disputes. Rather than attempt to split the difference, we are persuaded that, pursuant to Title VII and the ADA, whenever the EEOC chooses from among the many charges filed each year to bring an enforcement action in a particular case, the agency may be seeking to vindicate a public interest, not simply provide make-whole relief for the employee, even when it pursues entirely victim-specific relief. To hold otherwise would undermine the detailed enforcement scheme created by Congress simply to give greater effect to an agreement between private parties that does not even contemplate the EEOC's statutory function.

V.

It is true, as respondent and its amici have argued, that Baker's conduct may have the effect of limiting the relief that the EEOC may obtain in court. If, for example, he had failed to mitigate his damages, or had accepted a monetary settlement, any recovery by the EEOC would be limited accordingly. As we have noted, it "goes without saying that the courts can and should preclude double recovery by an individual." *General Telephone*, 446 U.S., at 333.

But no question concerning the validity of his claim or the character of the relief that could be appropriately awarded in either a judicial or an arbitral forum is presented by this record. Baker has not sought arbitration of his claim, nor is there any indication that he has entered into settlement negotiations with respondent. It is an open question whether a settlement or arbitration judgment would affect the validity of the EEOC's claim or the character of relief the EEOC may seek. The only issue before this Court is whether the fact that Baker has signed a mandatory arbitration agreement limits the remedies available to the EEOC. The text of the relevant statutes provides a clear answer to that question. They do not authorize the courts to balance the competing policies of the ADA and the FAA or to second-guess the agency's judgment concerning which of the remedies authorized by law that it shall seek in any given case. . . .

The judgment of the Court of Appeals is reversed, and the case is remanded for further proceedings consistent with this opinion.

Dissent by THOMAS, J., joined by REHNQUIST, C.J. and SCALIA, J.

B.

Not only would it be "inappropriate" for a court to allow the EEOC to obtain victim-specific relief on behalf of Baker, to do so in this case would contravene the "liberal federal policy favoring arbitration agreements" embodied in the FAA.

Under the terms of the FAA, Waffle House's arbitration agreement with Baker is valid and enforceable. The Court reasons, however, that the FAA is not implicated in this case because the EEOC was not a party to the arbitration agreement and "[i]t goes without saying that a contract cannot bind a nonparty." The Court's analysis entirely misses the point. The relevant question here is not whether the EEOC should be bound by Baker's agreement to arbitrate. Rather, it is whether a court should give effect to the arbitration agreement between Waffle House and Baker or whether it should instead allow the EEOC to reduce that arbitration agreement to all but a nullity. I believe that the FAA compels the former course.

By allowing the EEOC to pursue victim-specific relief on behalf of Baker under these circumstances, the Court eviscerates Baker's arbitration agreement with Waffle

House and liberates Baker from the consequences of his agreement. Waffle House gains nothing and, if anything, will be worse off in cases where the EEOC brings an enforcement action should it continue to utilize arbitration agreements in the future. This is because it will face the prospect of defending itself in two different forums against two different parties seeking precisely the same relief. It could face the EEOC in court and the employee in an arbitral forum.

The Court does not decide here whether an arbitral judgment would "affect the validity of the EEOC's claim or the character of relief the EEOC may seek" in court. Given the reasoning in the Court's opinion, however, the proverbial handwriting is on the wall. If the EEOC indeed is "the master of its own case," I do not see how an employee's independent decision to pursue arbitral proceedings could affect the validity of the "EEOC's claim" in court. Should this Court in a later case determine that an unfavorable arbitral judgment against an employee precludes the EEOC from seeking similar relief for that employee in court, then the Court's jurisprudence will stand for the following proposition: The EEOC may seek relief for an employee who has signed an arbitration agreement unless that employee decides that he would rather abide by his agreement and arbitrate his claim. Reconciling such a result with the FAA, however, would seem to be an impossible task and would make a mockery of the rationale underlying the Court's holding here: that the EEOC is "the master of its own case."

Assuming that the Court means what it says, an arbitral judgment will not preclude the EEOC's claim for victim-specific relief from going forward, and courts will have to adjust damages awards to avoid double recovery. If an employee, for instance, is able to recover $20,000 through arbitration and a court later concludes in an action brought by the EEOC that the employee is actually entitled to $100,000 in damages, one assumes that a court would only award the EEOC an additional $80,000 to give to the employee. Suppose, however, that the situation is reversed: An arbitrator awards an employee $100,000, but a court later determines that the employee is only entitled to $20,000 in damages. Will the court be required to order the employee to return $80,000 to his employer? I seriously doubt it.

==The Court's decision thus places those employers utilizing arbitration agreements at a serious disadvantage. Their employees will be allowed two bites at the apple—one in arbitration and one in litigation conducted by the EEOC—==and will be able to benefit from the more favorable of the two rulings. This result, however, discourages the use of arbitration agreements and is thus completely inconsistent with the policies underlying the FAA.

Victim-specific relief when employee has arbitrated or settled his or her claim. On the issue of monetary relief, the *Waffle House* Court acknowledged the lower courts' concern that plaintiffs might obtain double recovery—first through arbitration and then through EEOC-sponsored litigation. The Court made clear that plaintiffs should not be allowed double recovery by obtaining a favorable arbitration award and then receiving money from the EEOC as well. Yet because Baker did not pursue his claim in arbitration, the question of whether a settlement or arbitration award would adversely impact the validity of the EEOC's claim or the kind of relief the EEOC might seek remains open. For example, if an employee received an arbitration award for $100,000, with $20,000 allocated for backpay and $80,000 in punitive damages, should the EEOC be permitted to pursue both backpay and punitive damages on the employee's behalf in subsequent litigation with a required offset for sums the employee already received? Or should the EEOC be barred from bringing a claim because the employee has vindicated her rights in another forum? Another post–*Waffle House* issue might occur as follows: suppose an employee receives $100,000 in arbitration. Should the EEOC nevertheless be allowed to recover additional amounts for victim-specific relief? If it may do so, what should happen if the amount received by the EEOC differs from the amount received by the employee in arbitration? What if, for example, the EEOC recovers only $20,000 of victim-specific relief in court. Should the employee be required to return $80,000 of the arbitration award to the employer? The *Waffle House* dissenters view this as an unlikely possibility. Perhaps the employee should have to return $20,000 to the employer. Subsequent litigation on this issue seems inevitable.

Impact of EEOC settlements on subsequent arbitration. One issue that courts have not addressed is the effect of an EEOC settlement of an employee's claim for victim-specific relief on a subsequent arbitration between the employee and employer. In *Waffle House*, the Court was unequivocal that the EEOC has an independent right to sue and is not bound by the employee's arbitration agreement. Thus, the EEOC should not be precluded from settling claims, nor should an employee be barred from arbitrating even after the EEOC has settled a claim on his or her behalf. While an employer will surely introduce the fact of a settlement in a subsequent arbitration (assuming the settlement terms were not confidential), an arbitrator is not bound by the settlement in rendering his or her award. Of course, most arbitrators would consider the existing law on this issue prior to rendering a decision. Thus, a risk of double recovery remains only where an arbitrator ignores or is unaware of existing law.

Will employers abandon arbitration agreements in response to *Waffle House*? How frequently do these cases arise? The dissent suggests that the EEOC's ability to pursue victim-specific relief will discourage employers from adopting arbitration agreements because the *Waffle House* decision will allow the individual to pursue the employer in the arbitral forum while the EEOC pursues the employer in the judicial forum. The argument that allowing the EEOC to pursue backpay awards on behalf of employees who sign arbitration agreements would discourage employers from adopting arbitration agreements is unsupportable. The EEOC makes "for cause" determinations—that is, findings that sufficient evidence exists to conclude that the employee was the victim of discrimination—in very few of their cases. In 1994, only 2.69 percent of the cases (1,926 out of 71,563 cases) filed with the EEOC were found to be "for cause." Michael Selmi (1996) "The Value of the EEOC: Reexamining the Agency's Role in Employment Discrimination Law," 57 *Ohio St. L. J.* 1. Moreover, the EEOC does not file suit in all cases in which it enters a "for cause" determination. In 1994, it filed only 347 suits. Id. at 13. These numbers suggest that an employee would be extremely imprudent to place substantial hope on making an end run around his or her arbitration agreement. The likelihood that the EEOC would file a claim on the plaintiff's behalf is extremely low.

Impact on federal policy favoring arbitration. The argument that allowing the EEOC to pursue a claim on behalf of a plaintiff who previously agreed to arbitration would undermine the strong federal policy favoring arbitration is not particularly compelling either. The EEOC's position does not undermine arbitration; instead, it requires parties to use arbitration when they have contracted to do so. The EEOC merely contends that because it has independent authority to bring suit against an employer, it should be allowed to do so even when the employee is bound by an arbitration agreement. The EEOC's approach does not interfere with arbitration; it simply works within the arbitral system by allowing the EEOC to recover victim-specific relief only if the employee is unable to recover such relief through arbitration. The dissent's approach, which would prohibit the EEOC from pursuing any monetary relief, regardless of whether the individual employee has pursued her claims in arbitration and regardless of what she ultimately recovers, seems to do little more to further the federal policy favoring arbitration but quite a bit to undermine the EEOC's role in eliminating discrimination from the workplace.

Given the stated purpose of the EEOC—to vindicate the public interest in a workplace free of discrimination—the Court's decision not to take away the EEOC's power to punish employers with monetary penalties appears correct. The EEOC clearly views its monetary sanctions as a necessary weapon in its arsenal to create the proper incentives to eradicate discrimination in the workplace. Without monetary penalties, the EEOC's ability to protect the public interest in prohibiting employment discrimination would be impeded. Certainly in a case where the plaintiff makes no attempt to pursue her own remedies, or is limited in the remedies she may recover, no impediment should limit the EEOC's ability to seek monetary damages on her behalf.

E. FAIRNESS IN ARBITRAL PROCEDURE: WHO SHOULD PAY ARBITRATOR'S FEES?

In determining whether an arbitration agreement is unconscionable, courts typically examine the overall fairness of the agreement. See casebook pp. 252-263. Part of the determination of overall fairness turns on whether the agreement requires the plaintiff to pay part of the arbitrator's fees. The *Cole* court (casebook p. 258) suggested that such an arrangement would be unacceptable; the Due Process Protocol (casebook p. 254), by contrast, suggests that it is appropriate for an employee to pay part of the arbitrator's fees although it recommends that the employer pay for all fees if the employee is "lower paid." The California Supreme Court in *Armendariz v. Foundation Health Psychcare Services, Inc.*, 24 Cal. 4th 83 (Cal. 2000), stated that an arbitration agreement is unenforceable if it requires employees to pay either "unreasonable costs or any arbitrator's fees or expenses as a condition of access to the arbitration forum." See also *Maciejewski v. Alpha Systems Lab, Inc.*, 87 Cal. Rptr. 2d 390 (Cal. Ct. App. 1999) (appeals court refuses to enforce agreement requiring arbitration of age and race discrimination claims because requirement that employee pay half of the arbitrators' fees is unconscionable); but see *Zumpano v. Omnipoint Communications*, 2001 WL 43781 (E.D. Pa. Jan. 18, 2001) (arbitration agreement that may require employee to pay part of arbitrator's fees and expenses not per se unconscionable). Twin concerns appear to drive the jurisprudence on this issue; first, that the arbitrator's fees and the costs of the arbitration should be proportional to the value of the claim at issue and, second, that, in court, litigants do not have to pay the judge's fees or high filing fees. But see *Rosenberg v. Merrill Lynch*, 170 F.3d 1 (1st Cir. 1999) (court rejected employee's contention that arbitration agreement was unconscionable because it might subject him to forum fees as high as $3,000 per day); *Bradford v. Rockwell Semiconductor Systems*, 238 F.3d 549 (4th Cir. 2001) (arbitration agreement requiring employee and employer to share arbitration fees and costs is not per se unconscionable; court could conduct case-by-case analysis to determine whether the employee is able to pay the fees and costs and whether litigation costs would deter the employee from bringing a claim in court).

What happens when the parties' agreement is silent on the issue of who bears the costs of the arbitral process? In *Green Tree Financial Corp.—Alabama v. Randolph*, 531 U.S. 79 (2000), the Court considered whether Randolph, who had signed an arbitration agreement when she financed the purchase of a mobile home through Green Tree Financial, was obligated to arbitrate her Truth in Lending Act (TILA) and Equal Credit Opportunity Act claims. The Court concluded that she was and rejected her argument that the arbitration agreement's silence with respect to payment of filing fees, arbitrators' costs, and other arbitration expenses rendered the agreement unenforceable. The Court stated:

Chapter 4. Arbitration

In determining whether statutory claims may be arbitrated, we first ask whether the parties agreed to submit their claims to arbitration, and then ask whether Congress has evinced an intention to preclude a waiver of judicial remedies for the statutory rights at issue. See *Gilmer*, 111 S.Ct. 1647; *Mitsubishi*, 105 S.Ct. 3346. In this case, it is undisputed that the parties agreed to arbitrate all claims relating to their contract, including claims involving statutory rights.

Nor does Randolph contend that the TILA evinces an intention to preclude a waiver of judicial remedies. She contends instead that the arbitration agreement's silence with respect to costs and fees creates a "risk" that she will be required to bear prohibitive arbitration costs if she pursues her claims in an arbitral forum, and thereby forces her to forgo any claims she may have against petitioners. Therefore, she argues, she is unable to vindicate her statutory rights in arbitration. It may well be that the existence of large arbitration costs could preclude a litigant such as Randolph from effectively vindicating her federal statutory rights in the arbitral forum. But the record does not show that Randolph will bear such costs if she goes to arbitration. Indeed, it contains hardly any information on the matter. As the Court of Appeals recognized, "we lack . . . information about how claimants fare under Green Tree's arbitration clause." The record reveals only the arbitration agreement's silence on the subject, and that fact alone is plainly insufficient to render it unenforceable. The "risk" that Randolph will be saddled with prohibitive costs is too speculative to justify the invalidation of an arbitration agreement. . . .

To invalidate the agreement on that basis would undermine the "liberal federal policy favoring arbitration agreements." *Moses H. Cone Memorial Hospital*, 460 U.S., at 24. We have held that the party seeking to avoid arbitration bears the burden of establishing that Congress intended to preclude arbitration of the statutory claims at issue. See *Gilmer*, supra; *McMahon*, supra. Similarly, we believe that where, as here, a party seeks to invalidate an arbitration agreement on the ground that arbitration would be prohibitively expensive, that party bears the burden of showing the likelihood of incurring such costs.

Randolph did not meet that burden. How detailed the showing of prohibitive expense must be before the party seeking arbitration must come forward with contrary evidence is a matter we need not discuss; for in this case neither during discovery nor when the case was presented on the merits was there any timely showing at all on the point. The Court of Appeals therefore erred in deciding that the arbitration agreement's silence with respect to costs and fees rendered it unenforceable.[7]

---

7. We decline to reach respondent's argument that we may affirm the Court of Appeals' conclusion that the arbitration agreement is unenforceable on the alternative ground that the agreement precludes respondent from bringing her claims under the TILA as a class action.

Does it make sense for the Court to wait to rule on the question of whether the allocation of fees was proper until Randolph returns to court, following arbitration, if she contends that the ultimate cost allocation was prohibitively expensive? Does waiting serve the interest of judicial economy?

Question

4.11 Electronics International, a major electronics retailer with 30,000 employees in the United States, hired Martha Grainger as a sales associate at the rate of $12 per hour. At the time she began her employment, she signed an arbitration agreement that required her to pay half of the arbitrator's fee, currently $700 per day, and all of the arbitration's filing fee, $400. Martha has a sexual discrimination claim that she would like to file, but wonders whether these fees and costs can be avoided. Does *Randolph* provide any guidance on the question of whether an employee or consumer should have to shoulder the expense of hiring arbitrators or paying filing fees? What if the Electronics International arbitration agreement stated that "the loser pays" for the arbitrator's fees and the arbitration costs? Is that less problematic? One response to the *Randolph* case came from a major arbitrator provider, the National Arbitration Forum (NAF). Anticipating the need for redistribution of costs in light of *Randolph*, the NAF Code of Procedure shifts in large part the fees for small claims cases involving a dispute between an employer and employee or between a company and a consumer from employees and consumers to the company or employer.

F. CONTINUING ROLE OF STATE LAW IN ARBITRATION

A major tension in modern arbitration is the manner in which courts interpret seemingly contradictory state and federal arbitration law. For years, state legislatures have enacted legislation designed to exempt certain kinds of disputes from the coverage of state arbitration acts. Individual states have excluded from compliance with predispute arbitration agreements a wide variety of disputes, including non-union employer-employee disputes, disputes between an insured and an insurance company, and personal injury or other tort claims.

That states are exempting these categories is particularly interesting because Supreme Court case law makes abundantly clear that any state law that limits or invalidates contractual agreements to arbitrate is preempted by the (FAA) Federal Arbitration Act. Thus, the FAA preempts most state laws exempting categories of disputants from state arbitration act coverage, at least to the extent the transaction between the parties involved interstate commerce. Nevertheless, states continue to enact exceptions to the general rule enforcing arbitration agreements. It may be that these efforts are intended to be purely symbolic or that the states hope that by creating some consensus on categories of disputants deserving of additional protection, they might ultimately sway Congress to amend the FAA to exclude the protected categories of people.

The following section explores the continuing role of state legislation in the arbitration arena, focusing first on preemption and then on state legislative efforts to improve arbitral fairness.

1. Preemption

As arbitration has become more prevalent, the question of whether it is subject to state or federal regulation has arisen on several occasions. As discussed above, the Supreme Court's jurisprudence in this area mandates that state law, to the extent that it conflicts with the FAA, is preempted. Thus, state legislation that prohibited arbitration of franchisee-franchisor disputes was preempted, as was state legislation that required "waiver of the right to sue in court" provisions contained in consumer contracts to appear in larger print. See *Southland Corp. v. Keating*, 465 U.S. 2 (1984), and *Doctor's Associates v. Cassarotto*, 517 U.S. 681 (1996). Both state laws were viewed as inconsistent with the policy articulated in the FAA that precludes states from treating arbitration agreements differently from other kinds of contracts. See casebook p. 252.

In its recent term, the Supreme Court contemplated the preemption issue again, albeit indirectly. In *Circuit City v. Adams*, 121 S. Ct. 1302 (2001), an employee, Saint Clair Adams, filed an employment discrimination lawsuit against Circuit City in state court. Circuit City sought to compel arbitration of Adams's claims in federal court based on the broad arbitration agreement Adams had signed at the time he applied for his job. The Court considered whether section 1 of the FAA, which excludes from the Act's coverage "contracts of employment of seamen, railroad employees, or any other class of workers engaged in foreign or interstate commerce" should be interpreted narrowly, exempting from coverage only contracts of employment of transportation workers, or broadly, so that all contracts of employment are beyond the FAA's reach. Answering the question posed in *Circuit City* impacts the state's role in regulating arbitration because state law affecting arbitration of employment disputes would be preempted if the exclusion in FAA section 1 were broadly construed, but not if it was narrowly construed.

In what was essentially a statutory interpretation debate, the *Circuit City* Court considered the plain language of section 1 of the FAA:

> If . . . there is an argument to be made that arbitration agreements in employment contracts are not covered by the Act, it must be premised on the language of the

§1 exclusion provision itself. Respondent, endorsing the reasoning of the Court of Appeals for the Ninth Circuit that the provision excludes all employment contracts, relies on the asserted breadth of the words "contracts of employment of . . . any other class of workers engaged in . . . commerce." Referring to our construction of §2's coverage provision in *Allied-Bruce*—concluding that the words "involving commerce" evidence the congressional intent to regulate to the full extent of its commerce power—respondent contends §1's interpretation should have a like reach, thus exempting all employment contracts. The two provisions, it is argued, are coterminous; under this view the "involving commerce" provision brings within the FAA's scope all contracts within the Congress' commerce power, and the "engaged in . . . commerce" language in §1 in turn exempts from the FAA all employment contracts falling within that authority.

This reading of §1, however, runs into an immediate and, in our view, insurmountable textual obstacle. Unlike the "involving commerce" language in §2, the words "any other class of workers engaged in . . . commerce" constitute a residual phrase, following, in the same sentence, explicit reference to "seamen" and "railroad employees." Construing the residual phrase to exclude all employment contracts fails to give independent effect to the statute's enumeration of the specific categories of workers which precedes it; there would be no need for Congress to use the phrases "seamen" and "railroad employees" if those same classes of workers were subsumed within the meaning of the "engaged in . . . commerce" residual clause. The wording of §1 calls for the application of the maxim *ejusdem generis*, the statutory canon that "[w]here general words follow specific words in a statutory enumeration, the general words are construed to embrace only objects similar in nature to those objects enumerated by the preceding specific words." 2A N. Singer, Sutherland on Statutes and Statutory Construction §47.17 (1991). Under this rule of construction the residual clause should be read to give effect to the terms "seamen" and "railroad employees," and should itself be controlled and defined by reference to the enumerated categories of workers which are recited just before it; the interpretation of the clause pressed by respondent fails to produce these results.

The dissenters in the 5-4 decision suggested that the Court consider the scope of congressional authority to regulate under the commerce power at the time the FAA was enacted:

Times have changed. Judges in the 19th century disfavored private arbitration. The 1925 Act was intended to overcome that attitude, but a number of this Court's cases decided in the last several decades have pushed the pendulum far beyond a neutral attitude and endorsed a policy that strongly favors private arbitration. The strength of that policy preference has been echoed in the recent Court of Appeals opinions on which the Court relies. In a sense, therefore, the

Court is standing on its own shoulders when it points to those cases as the basis for its narrow construction of the exclusion in §1. There is little doubt that the Court's interpretation of the Act has given it a scope far beyond the expectations of the Congress that enacted it. . . .

It is not necessarily wrong for the Court to put its own imprint on a statute. But when its refusal to look beyond the raw statutory text enables it to disregard countervailing considerations that were expressed by Members of the enacting Congress and that remain valid today, the Court misuses its authority. As the history of the legislation indicates, the potential disparity in bargaining power between individual employees and large employers was the source of organized labor's opposition to the Act, which it feared would require courts to enforce unfair employment contracts. That same concern . . . underlay Congress' exemption of contracts of employment from mandatory arbitration. When the Court simply ignores the interest of the unrepresented employee, it skews its interpretation with it own policy preferences.

The *Circuit City* majority quickly rejected this argument, stating that

[a] variable standard for interpreting common, jurisdictional phrases would contradict our earlier cases and bring instability to statutory interpretation. The Court has declined in past cases to afford significance, in construing the meaning of the statutory jurisdictional provisions 'in commerce' and 'engaged in commerce,' to the circumstance that the statute predated shifts in the Court's Commerce Clause cases.

Questions

4.12 Will *Circuit City* increase the likelihood that employers will require their employees to sign arbitration agreements as a condition of employment?

4.13 What impact does an arbitration agreement have on the ability of a group of employees to bring a class action challenging the use of mandatory arbitration agreements or the manner in which they are administered? Does the *Circuit City* ruling encourage employees to overcome their collective action problems?

4.14 What if a consumer of cellular phone service filed a class action alleging that the phone service company wrongfully billed long-distance fees and the next day received in the mail her bill and a pamphlet that restated many of the original terms and conditions of her service contract together with a newly effective arbitration agreement? What if the arbitration agreement came the day before she filed her lawsuit? See *Powertel, Inc. v. Bexley*, 743 So. 2d 570 (Fla. Dist. Ct. App. 1999) (court did not enforce arbitration agreement received day after lawsuit filed both because it was retroactive and because it was unconscionable since it deprived plaintiff of the ability to file class action); *In re Knepp*, 229 Bankr. 921 (N.D. Ala.

1999) (arbitration agreement that interferes with ability to bring class actions is unconscionable); *but see Randolph v. Green Tree Financial Corp.*, 244 F.3d 814 (11th Cir. 2001) (agreement authorizing arbitration of TILA claims enforceable even though it precludes class actions). Some courts are willing to order class actions to arbitration. The question then is whether the case will be handled as a class action in arbitration or whether the parties must proceed individually in arbitration. See Jean R. Sternlight (2000) "As Mandatory Binding Arbitration Meets the Class Action, Will the Class Action Survive?" 42 *Wm. & Mary L. Rev.* 1, 65. State law may permit consolidation of arbitrations, thus allowing a court to order classwide arbitration. See Jacqueline E. Mottek (Nov. 28, 2000) "The Impact of Mandatory Arbitration Clauses on Class Certification," 69 *U.S.L.W.* 2307. Professor Sternlight suggests that existing federal statutes and traditional contract law should, under certain circumstances, prohibit companies from using arbitration agreements to preclude individual plaintiffs from bringing class actions. Sternlight at 78. Based on the Supreme Court's current attitude toward the enforceability of arbitration agreements, how might a plaintiff who has signed a broad arbitration agreement fare if she files a class action in court based on violations of Title VII? Would the court void the arbitration agreement? Would it order the case to arbitration on an individual basis? Or would it order the arbitrator to hear the claims as a class action? Should Congress pass legislation prohibiting the use of arbitration agreements to eliminate the ability to bring class actions? Sternlight suggests that it should. Id. at 121.

4.15 Should a court ordering parties to participate in classwide arbitration remain involved in the arbitral process? Traditionally, once a court orders parties to arbitration, the court's involvement ceases until the stage where one of the parties requests judicial review of the arbitral award. Should this practice be applied in the classwide arbitration context? Who should make initial determinations regarding certification and notice? What about the rights of absent class members?

4.16 In 1997, the EEOC issued its Policy Statement on Mandatory Arbitration of Employment Disputes as a Condition of Employment. See 133 D.L.R. E-4 (July 11, 1997). The statement articulated the EEOC's belief that mandatory pre-dispute arbitration agreements are inconsistent with United States civil rights laws. Reiterating the importance of the nation's civil rights laws, the EEOC offered several reasons why the inherent limitations of mandatory arbitration make it an inappropriate mechanism for resolving employment disputes. First, emphasizing that the arbitral process is private in nature, the EEOC criticized arbitration because it allows for minimal public accountability and inhibits the development of the law. Second, the EEOC emphasized that the structure of arbitration is biased against the employee. According to the EEOC, the arbitral process provides innumerable benefits to the repeat player employer at the expense of the one-shot employee. For example, the repeat player employer has systematic advantages both in negotiating the arbitration agreement and in selecting the arbitrator because (1) the employer drafts the

Chapter 4. Arbitration
Page 269

agreement, garnering the lion's share of the benefits for itself; (2) it has more knowledge both about the process itself and the arbitrators who may preside over hearings; and (3) it has the incentive and opportunity to facilitate informal relationships with those arbitrators. In the EEOC's view, these advantages render the arbitral process irretrievably suspect.

Do you agree with the EEOC's position? Why can't potential plaintiffs obtain sufficient information about arbitrators prior to the arbitration so as to ensure that the arbitrator ultimately selected is unbiased or biased in the employee's favor? Couldn't a group of plaintiffs' attorneys develop an accessible shared database of information about prospective arbitrators? Would such an effort make sense? Shouldn't an employee be able to negotiate around an arbitration agreement if he or she is really opposed to it? How successful do you think such negotiations would be?

Why does it appear that employees (and the EEOC) are opposed to arbitration? Are the true opponents of arbitration the attorneys who currently represent employees in judicial proceedings? What advantages might arbitration hold for an employee? In answering this question consider the views of the following commentators. In "The Changing Role of Labor Arbitration," 76 *Ind. L.J.* 83, 91-93 (2001), Professor Theodore J. St. Antoine suggests that lower-paid employees might be better off in mandatory arbitration than in litigation because they might have an opportunity to litigate their case and they might receive a better recovery than they would in court:

> Experienced plaintiffs' attorneys have estimated that only about five percent of the individuals with an employment claim who seek help from the private bar are able to obtain counsel. One of the Detroit area's top employment specialists was more precise in a conversation with me. His secretary kept an actual count; he took on only one out of eighty-seven persons who contacted him for possible representation. Now, many of those who are rejected will not have meritorious claims. But others will be workers whose potential dollar recovery will simply not justify the investment of the time and money of a first-rate lawyer in preparing a court action. For those individuals, the cheaper, simpler process of arbitration is the most feasible recourse. It will cost a lawyer far less time and effort to take a case to arbitration; at worst, claimants can represent themselves or be represented by laypersons in this much less formal and intimidating forum....
>
> Even if individual claimants can get to court, mounting empirical evidence indicates most of them will fare less well there than they would before a qualified arbitrator. Several studies show that employees actually win more often in arbitration than in court and, while a successful plaintiff recovers more from a judge and a jury, claimants as a group get more from arbitrators. That was true before the due-process protocol was adopted, and should be even truer with the protocol in effect. Most court dockets are heavily backlogged and delay is endemic. That can be devastating for the fired worker without a job or with a much-reduced

income. A considerably more conservative judiciary than existed in earlier years may be all too willing to grant summary judgment against those civil-rights plaintiffs who do manage to file suit. Traditional labor arbitrators have had to remain mutually acceptable to unions and employers, and the same is likely to become true for arbitrators in the new employer/individual-employee field as an increasingly savvy plaintiffs' bar develops. There is no comparable check on the lifetime appointees to the federal bench or, as a practical matter, on longtime incumbents of state courts.

Not all commentators agree with Professor St. Antoine. For example, Professor Lisa Bingham conducted a study of 270 cases consisting of arbitration awards decided in 1993 under the AAA Commercial Arbitration Rules and arbitration awards decided in 1993 and 1994 under the AAA Employment Dispute Rules. Lisa B. Bingham (1997) "Employment Arbitration: The Repeat Player Effect," 1 *Employee Rts. & Employment Poly. J.* 189, 206 (hereinafter Bingham, *Employment Arbitration*). This study, which reviewed awards rendered prior to the implementation of the Due Process Protocol, revealed that arbitrators award damages to employees less frequently and in lower amounts when the employer is a repeat player. Bingham, *Employment Arbitration* at 209-210. According to Professor Bingham, in repeat player cases, employees recover only 11 percent of what they demand; while in cases against nonrepeat player employers, they recover approximately 48 percent of what they demand. Lisa Bingham (1998) "On Repeat Players, Adhesive Contracts, and the Use of Statistics in Judicial Review of Employment Arbitration Awards," 29 *McGeorge L. Rev.* 223, 234 (hereinafter Bingham, *On Repeat Players*). Moreover, employees lose significantly more often in cases involving repeat player employers. Bingham, *Employment Arbitration* at 209. According to the study, employees arbitrating with one-shot player employers win over 70 percent of the time. When arbitrating against repeat player employers, however, they win only 16 percent of the time. Bingham, *On Repeat Players* at 234.

More recently, Professor Bingham examined the Due Process Protocol's impact on arbitrations between one-shot and repeat players. Her examination offers additional support to the theory that employers have structural advantages in the arbitration process by virtue of their repeat player status. Bingham, *Employment Arbitration* at 215. Although her study of arbitrations using the Protocol suggests that the adoption of the Protocol lessens the impact of the employer's repeat player status, it certainly does not suggest that the advantage is eliminated. In fact, Professor Bingham reports that only when both the Protocol and a personnel handbook are adopted does the employer's likelihood of success decrease. Bingham could not support her hypothesis that the Protocol alone reduces the chances of employer success.

4.17 Prior to the *Circuit City* decision, every federal appeals court except the Ninth Circuit had held that the FAA covers employment contracts. The Ninth Circuit

Chapter 4. Arbitration

also stands alone in its position that mandatory arbitration agreements do not bind employees who have claims under Title VII of the 1964 Civil Rights Act. See *Duffield v. Robertson Stephens & Co.*, 144 F.3d 1182 (9th Cir. 1998). In *Duffield*, the Ninth Circuit considered the legislative history of the 1991 Civil Rights Act, which encouraged the use of alternative dispute resolution, including arbitration, "where appropriate and to the extent authorized by law." The primary issue was whether the law at the time the Civil Rights Act of 1991 was enacted authorized or precluded the use of arbitration to resolve Title VII claims. The court concluded that because *Alexander v. Gardner-Denver* was still good law at the time the Act was enacted and *Gardner-Denver* held that employees could not be required to arbitrate Title VII claims, Congress's use of the language was intended to codify its position that compulsory arbitration of Title VII claims was neither appropriate nor authorized by law. Is *Duffield* still good law in the Ninth Circuit following the Court's *Circuit City* holding? No

2. The Revised Uniform Arbitration Act

Attempting to bridge the gap in arbitral fairness without triggering preemption, in 2000 the National Conference of Commissioners on Uniform State Laws (NCCUSL) unanimously adopted major revisions to the Uniform Arbitration Act, the first such revisions since the Act was promulgated in 1955. The UAA had been the law in 49 jurisdictions. Already adopted by New Mexico, Hawaii, Utah and Nevada and under consideration by a number of other states, the Revised Uniform Arbitration Act (RUAA) attempts to address arbitral developments created by an extraordinary increase in the use of arbitration and the resulting legal questions associated with the increased use. See Timothy J. Heinsz (2001) "The Revised Uniform Arbitration Act: Modernizing, Revising, and Clarifying Arbitration Law," 2001 *J. of Dis. Res.* 1.

The RUAA (Appendix H), like the Due Process Protocol before it, tends to judicialize arbitration. Admitting that its primary objective is to enhance procedural protections in the arbitral process, the drafters emphasize that many of the RUAA's provisions are nonwaivable or nonwaivable until a dispute arises to ensure that "fundamental fairness to the parties will be preserved, particularly in those instances where one party may have significantly less bargaining power than another." RUAA at i. Those provisions that cannot be waived until a dispute arises include the right to representation by an attorney at an arbitral proceeding, the right to move the arbitrator to award provisional remedies and interim awards, and the right to move the arbitrator to issue subpoenas for witnesses and records or to order depositions. See RUAA §§4, 8, 17(a), 17(c). The nonwaivable provisions focus on the parties' ability to waive the court's participation in the arbitral process. Thus, the nonwaivable provisions include those that prohibit parties from waiving the right to move the court to confirm, vacate, or modify an arbitral award or compel or stay arbitration; the power of the court to award reasonable costs for motions and subsequent judicial proceedings; and arbitrator immunity or the arbitrator's right not to testify. Id. at §4(c).

Concern about preemption issues prompted RUAA drafters to limit the scope of the Act to the arbitral process itself. Id. at 14 ("treating arbitration clauses differently from other contractual provisions would raise significant preemption issues under the Federal Arbitration Act"). Limitations or restrictions of parties' ability to enter into an agreement to arbitrate would, in the view of the drafters, be preempted by the FAA. Id. at ii. Although the drafters were less clear about the preemptive impact of the FAA on the provisions governing judicial review of arbitral awards, the drafters, in an earlier draft of the RUAA, nevertheless cautiously approached this issue, eschewing the notion that judicial review of an arbitral award could be granted on grounds other than those articulated in FAA section 10. RUAA draft at 47-52 (Feb. 2000). For further discussion of the question of whether section 10's provisions are default or mandatory rules, see Sarah Rudolph Cole (2000) "Managerial Litigants? The Overlooked Problem of Party Autonomy in Dispute Resolution," 51 *Hastings L.J.* 1199.

The RUAA's focus on governance of arbitration issues was driven by the drafters' belief that the FAA is unlikely to preempt state rules focusing on the workings of the arbitral mechanism. Id. at iii. Unlike questions regarding the enforceability of the agreement to arbitrate or the question of arbitral award review, Congress, in drafting the FAA, left the arbitral process largely unregulated. The Supreme Court confirmed this theory in *Volt Information Sciences, Inc. v. Leland Stanford University,* 498 U.S. 468 (1989), when it held that state law principles selected by the parties to govern their arbitration will not be preempted by the FAA as long as they do not interfere with the enforceability of the arbitration agreement. Thus, the RUAA's focus on regulating the arbitral process rather than the negotiation of the arbitration agreement makes sense.

Questions

4.18 By making extensive discovery available and unwaivable until the dispute arises, does the RUAA impose too heavy a burden on traditional arbitrations, often defined as arbitration among repeat players? Are there sufficient countervailing benefits so that the imposition of procedural burdens on two repeat players can be justified?

4.19 Does the RUAA's judicialization of the arbitral process provide sufficient protection to one-shot players compelled by predispute arbitration agreements to arbitrate their statutory claims?

The RUAA is not the only legislative effort designed to remedy the perceived disadvantages one-shot players experience when negotiating an arbitration clause and participating in arbitration with a repeat player. Members of Congress have proposed amendments to exempt certain kinds of disputes from the FAA rather than reforming the FAA to provide due process protections where there is perceived unfairness. The congressional approach is troublesome because the potential exemptions to the FAA are proposed primarily by interest groups with strong lobbies. As a result, to the extent that certain kinds of disputes are ultimately exempted from the FAA's provisions, it is likely that those exemptions will do little to help the true one-shot players like the employee and the consumer.

An example of this approach is the proposed legislation titled *The Fairness and Voluntary Arbitration Act*. H.R. 534, 106th Cong., 1st Sess. (1999). This act, which currently has 238 cosponsors in the House of Representatives and was approved unanimously by the House Judiciary Committee, would amend the FAA to exempt from its coverage predispute arbitration agreements between car dealers and manufacturers. A similar bill in the Senate, the *Motor Vehicle Franchise Contract Arbitration Fairness Act,* would prohibit car manufacturers from requiring car and truck dealers to sign predispute arbitration agreements as a condition of doing business. Underlying the effort to pass these bills is the belief that the difference in bargaining power between automobile dealers and manufacturers is so significant that enforcing a predispute arbitration agreement would be unconscionable. While car dealers may be at some disadvantage in negotiations with car manufacturers, they are hardly the one-shot players most in need of federal legislative protection. Ironically, while the car dealers attempt to obtain this exemption for dealings with car manufacturers, they continue to include in their contracts with consumers predispute agreements to arbitrate any controversies arising out of automobile sales.

More comprehensive legislation has been proposed that would amend the various antidiscrimination statutes, including Title VII of the Civil Rights Act of 1964, the Age Discrimination in Employment Act of 1967, the Americans with Disabilities Act of 1990, Section 1981, the Fair Labor Standards Act of 1938, and the Family and Medical Leave Act of 1993. H.R. 872, 106th Cong., 1st Sess. (1999). The bill would prohibit predispute arbitration agreements involving claims of employment discrimination based on race, color, sex, national origin, religion, age, and disability. Similar legislation has been introduced in the Senate. The Senate bill would also amend the FAA to exclude claims of unlawful employment discrimination. (S. 121, 106th Cong., 1st Sess. (1999).)

The RUAA addresses a variety of other issues as well. In addition to anticipating e-commerce arbitration, the RUAA authorizes arbitrators to award provisional remedies as well as attorneys' fees and punitive damages (to the extent authorized by law in a civil action regarding the same claim). The RUAA also requires for the first time that arbitrators disclose actual or apparent conflicts of interest (RUAA §12) and confers on arbitrators immunity from civil liability to the same extent as a judge (RUAA §14). Moreover, the RUAA grants arbitrators discretion to order prehearing discovery but cautions arbitrators to use that power appropriately in the circumstances by balancing parties' needs with the interest in ensuring a fair and efficient dispute resolution process. (RUAA §17.)

4.20 Four states have adopted the RUAA: Hawaii, Nevada, Utah and New Mexico. Hawaii adopted the Act unchanged. Nevada's version of the RUAA does not grant arbitrators the power to award punitive damages. New Mexico's version includes a provision that limits the ability of repeat players to utilize arbitration agreements with one-shot players. According to the law, a "disabling civil dispute clause[s]," defined as a "provision modifying or limiting procedural rights necessary or useful to a consumer, borrower, tenant, or employee in the enforcement of substantive rights" against another party, is unenforceable. What kinds of procedural rights are necessary or useful to a consumer? Will this law survive a challenge that it is preempted by the FAA?

4.21 Ohio Computer Group, a small company that conducts business only in Ohio, wants to include in its employment contracts with its employees a predispute agreement to arbitrate. In that agreement, the company would like to limit employees suing under antidiscrimination statutes to obtaining backpay damages. Would such a limitation be permissible under the RUAA?

Congress and the states are not alone in their efforts to increase fairness in the arbitration process. Perhaps because they are tired of waiting for effective legislative efforts, some arbitral repeat players are negotiating among themselves for changes to the arbitral process. The parties are not relying on the arbitral process alone to improve fairness; instead, they rely on the court system as the enforcement mechanism to ensure that efforts to increase quality and fairness in arbitration are achieved. The most prominent method parties have selected to improve fairness in arbitration is to contract for expanded judicial review of arbitral awards. While some courts have expressed a willingness to adopt the parties' proposed standards for judicial review, other courts have refused. Compare *Lapine Tech Corp. v. Kyocera Corp.*, 130 F.3d 884 (9th Cir. 1997) (court enforced party agreement to review arbitral award for errors of law), with *Bowen v. Amoco Pipeline Co.*, 254 F.3d 925 (10th Cir. 2001) (parties cannot contractually alter FAA standard for judicial review).

The question of whether, and to what extent, litigant control over the dispute resolution process in the judicial setting is appropriate is a question that has been largely ignored. While arbitration and other ADR processes are traditionally private processes in which parties experience substantial autonomy, courts, by contrast, are public institutions designed to serve a public function. Parties' attempts to obtain nontraditional exercises of judicial power, then, may jeopardize the courts' institutional integrity. Courts need a reliable and consistent framework for evaluating the various requests parties make and for determining which they will adopt and which they must deny. Professor Sarah Rudolph Cole has proposed such a test, designed for any request for nontraditional judicial involvement in dispute resolution. First, the court evaluating the request should consider whether Congress granted the court the authority to approve the parties' requests. Second, the court must consider

Chapter 4. Arbitration

whether approval of the parties' requests will impermissibly undermine the institutional integrity of the court. Application of this second test may require consideration of the impact on third parties, judicial resources, and the court's institutional stature. See Sarah Rudolph Cole (2000) "Managerial Litigants? The Overlooked Problem of Party Autonomy in Dispute Resolution," 51 *Hastings L.J.* 1199, 1205-1206. For further discussion of this issue, see casebook p. 414.

4.22 Will the two-part test work effectively? Imagine that the parties have agreed that a court will review an arbitration award by treating it like a lower court opinion or by rendering a decision with regard only to industry custom, not law. Should a judge enforce such an agreement? What impact might that have on the judiciary as a whole? Does the FAA §10 (judicial review provision) allow parties to agree to expand judicial review?

G. ARBITRATION ETHICS

The increasing rate of arbitration agreement implementation, particularly by employers and businesses in their relationships with employees and consumers, has focused attention on the character and scope of the ethical obligations of arbitral provider organizations. In 2000, the CPR-Georgetown Commission on Ethics and Standards of Practice in ADR released for comment draft principles for ADR Provider Organizations — that is, those organizations that make available neutrals to preside over the variety of available ADR methods. These principles provide, among other things, that ADR Provider Organizations, including arbitral provider organizations, make reasonable efforts to maximize the quality and competence of their services; provide information about their services and organization to potential clients; ensure that they administer ADR processes that are "fundamentally fair and conducted in an impartial manner"; provide services of reasonable cost to low-income parties; protect confidentiality by taking "all reasonable steps to protect the level of confidentiality agreed to by the parties, established by the organization or neutral, or set by applicable law or contract"; and disclose conflicts of interest "reasonably likely to affect the impartiality or independence" of the organization or that might create the appearance that the organization is biased against one party or favorable to another. For a thorough discussion of these rules see Carrie Menkel-Meadow (2001) "Ethics in ADR: The Many "Cs" of Professional Responsibility and Dispute Resolution," 28 *Fordham Urb. L.J.* 979; Margaret L. Shaw and Elizabeth Plapinger (2001) "Ethical Guidelines — ADR Provider Organizations Should Increase Transparency, Disclosure," *Dis. Res. Mag.* 14 (Spring).

Principle V, the provision on conflict of interest disclosure, has garnered attention from critics of mandatory arbitration. See Cliff Palefsky (2001) "Only a

Start: ADR Provider Ethics Principles Don't Go Far Enough," *Dis. Res. Mag.* 19 (Spring). Principle V states:

> a. The ADR Provider Organization should disclose the existence of any interests or relationships which are reasonably likely to affect the impartiality or independence of the Organization or which might reasonably create the appearance that the Organization is biased against a party or favorable to another, including (i) any financial or other interest by the Organization in the outcome; (ii) any significant financial, business, organizational, professional or other relationship that the Organization has with any of the parties or their counsel, including a contractual stream of referrals, a de facto stream of referrals, or a funding relationship between a party and the organization; or (iii) any other significant source of bias or prejudice concerning the Organization which is reasonably likely to affect impartiality or might reasonably create an appearance of partiality or bias.

The principle requires that an ADR provider organization make reasonable efforts to avoid partiality or the appearance of partiality through a process of disclosure to the parties. Although the principle requires that the organization disclose financial interests in the outcome of a dispute, critics suggest that organizations, particularly arbitral provider organizations, will not provide disclosure sufficient to remedy the problems created by a system that is already biased in favor of corporate repeat players. In arbitration particularly, major arbitral providers solicit big businesses, either directly or through an arbitrator on the providers' panel list, to include arbitral provisions in their employment or business contracts and to list the provider as the arbitrator for disputes that might arise. Does Principle V require that this information be disclosed to parties at the time they select an arbitrator? Critics worry that organizations will interpret the principle narrowly, so that disclosure in this context would not be required even though, in the critics' view, it would create an appearance of bias.

No jurisdiction has adopted the Draft Principles, so they do not have the force of law. Is there any incentive for an organization to represent that it will abide by these rules?

Questions

4.23 Imagine that *ABC*, an arbitral provider organization located in State *X*, asks its corporate clients (i.e., those it already provides services to) to join *ABC* at different levels of membership that range in cost from $5,000 to $50,000. In exchange for becoming a member of *ABC*, *ABC* will offer special instruction in arbitral and mediation advocacy as well as discounts on fees and services. Is this arrangement ethical? Should this arrangement be disclosed if State *X* adopts Principle V of the CPR-Georgetown rules?

4.24 Commentators have criticized the American Arbitration Association (AAA) for engaging in the following activities: (1) submitting an amicus brief on behalf of Circuit City in *Circuit City v. Saint Clair Adams*, 121 S. Ct. 1302 (2001), in which the Court held that employment agreements between employers and employees were enforceable under the FAA; and (2) asking AAA arbitrators to identify corporations where they had contacts so that AAA marketing representatives could contact those corporations to seek business and provide training. If AAA were to adopt the proposed CPR-Georgetown rules, would they be able to engage in these practices? Should ethical rules prevent arbitral organizations like AAA from engaging in these practices?

Page 269. Add the following References:

BINGHAM, Lisa B. (1997) "Employment Arbitration: The Repeat Player Effect," 1 *Employee Rts. & Emp. Poly. J.* 189, 206.

BINGHAM, Lisa B. (1998) "On Repeat Players, Adhesive Contracts, and the Use of Statistics in Judicial Review of Employment Arbitration Awards," 29 *McGeorge L. Rev.* 223, 234.

COLE, Sarah Rudolph (2000) "Managerial Litigants? The Overlooked Problem of Party Autonomy in Dispute Resolution," 51 *Hastings L.J.* 1199.

HEINSZ, Timothy J. (2001) "The Revised Uniform Arbitration Act: Modernizing, Revising, and Clarifying Arbitration Law," 2001 *J. of Disp. Res.* 1.

MENKEL-MEADOW, Carrie (2001) "Ethics in ADR: The Many "Cs" of Professional Responsibility and Dispute Resolution," 28 *Fordham Urb. L.J.* 979.

MOTTEK, Jacqueline E. (2000) "The Impact of Mandatory Arbitration Clauses on Class Certification," 69 *U.S.L.W.* 2307.

PALEFSKY, Cliff (2001) "Only a Start: ADR Provider Ethics Principles Don't Go Far Enough," *Dis. Res. Mag.* 19 (Spring).

SELMI, Michael (1996) "The Value of the EEOC: Reexamining the Agency's Role in Employment Discrimination Law," 57 *Ohio St. L.J.* 1.

SHAW, Margaret L., and Elizabeth PLAPINGER (2001) "Ethical Guidelines—ADR Provider Organizations Should Increase Transparency, Disclosure," *Dis. Res. Mag.* 14 (Spring).

ST. ANTOINE, Theodore J. (2001) "The Changing Role of Labor Arbitration," 76 *Ind. L.J.* 83, 91-93.

STERNLIGHT, Jean R. (2000) "As Mandatory Binding Arbitration Meets the Class Action, Will the Class Action Survive?," 42 *Wm. & Mary L. Rev.* 1, 65.

5
COMBINING AND APPLYING THE BASIC PROCESSES

C. RECOMMENDING A PROCESS FOR A CASE

Page 311. **Insert Before the Questions:**

For a detailed discussion of diagnosing a case for ADR, see Edward Dauer (2000) *Alternative Dispute Resolution and Practice* ch. 6 (Juris. Publishers).

D. REPRESENTING A CLIENT IN DISPUTE RESOLUTION

1. Premediation

Page 317. With the excerpt by Deanne Siemer, compare the following piece reflecting her revised views ten years later. What might account for the different emphases now?

PERSPECTIVES OF ADVOCATES AND CLIENTS ON COURT-SPONSORED ADR

1. Envisioning Information

The incomparable Edward Tufte says: "The world is complex, dynamic, multi-dimensional; the paper is static, flat. How are we to represent the rich visual world of experience and measurement on mere flatland?"[1] Mediation often presents the first real demands on the lawyer to translate long hours of fact investigation into a few graphics that will help carry the central message to the mediator and the other side in relatively short presentation. Complicated legal theories may need diagrammatic representations to lead the mediator through the maze.

Persuasion in any legal forum is increasingly about envisioning information, and this is not easy work. Tailoring graphics for mediation requires a sense about persuasion for compromise, which can be quite different from persuasion for combat. If one side shows up at the mediation with effective information displays, either on paper or video screen, the other side usually will be at a disadvantage. Mediators, like judges, think they are not affected by good graphics but in fact much prefer looking at pictures to reading words. Mediators absorb information much more quickly and accurately when it is delivered with well-designed graphics.

Lawyers who understand this dynamic worry about the cost of the thinking time that needs to go into mediation graphics.

2. Distending Case Theory

Trials resolve factual disputes. Mediation in cases headed for trial (and not summary judgment on questions of law) brings together two or more parties, each of whom, if they are adequately prepared for trial, have a case theory. The case theory has been constructed to account for all of the "known" facts, accord with common sense, and to be told by credible witnesses. The case theory consists of admissible evidence and contains all the elements of a cause of action or defense.

Mediation usually does not stay within the case theory. It takes account of unvarnished hearsay, moseys into subjects that will have no place in the presentation at trial, and allows much more story-telling advocacy by counsel. This requires counsel to respond in a persuasive way, while sticking to the case theory that ultimately is the reason to believe there will be a favorable outcome at trial.

Lawyers sometimes worry about the client, who may later have to testify, being distracted from an effective presentation by recalling points made by the mediator.

3. Monetizing Harms and Benefits

The harms and benefits discussed in a mediation may go well beyond the assertions of the complaint and answer or counterclaim. Normally, established economic methods are available to monetize these harms and benefits so that everyone at the table is talking in the same terms. However, the mediator may not have the skills

---

1. Tufte, Edward R., *Envisioning Information*, Graphics Press, Cheshire, Ct. 1990, p. 9.

necessary to apply these methods as they have become increasingly mathematical in nature. If the mediator cannot deal with the math or formulae, sophisticated clients may lose confidence.

Another aspect of this problem has to do with fees. Lawyers working under contingent fee arrangements are sensitive about revealing either their percentage entitlements or their likely costs to complete trial. Lawyers working on hourly fee arrangements also are reluctant about discussions of litigation costs as they may not have had any realistic discussions with the client about cost, or their estimates may have been made some time ago while in the grip of optimism. Mediators view savings of preparation and trial costs as a useful perspective on settlement. For that reason, they usually try to get realistic numbers on the table and sometimes suggest their own. These estimates may be a surprise to the client and may cause anxiety about the process.

4. Exposing the Client

Some clients are fairly unappealing, either as people or as representatives of organizations. When the mediator calls upon a client to state views or respond to questions, the protection of the lawyer as spokesperson is stripped away. Lawyers believe, based on considerable experience, that unattractive clients will affect the approach of the mediator as to an appropriate outcome for a settlement, perhaps giving an advantage to the other side.

Unappealing people can do reasonably well in the structured setting of witness examination. They can learn to answer questions on direct and cross examination with just the facts, unadorned by their perhaps sexist, racist, or otherwise unfortunate philosophical outlooks. In a dispute, for example about a promissory note, the court may not ever be distracted by the client's approach to life. It is much more difficult to prepare such clients to speak well at mediations where the discussion may drift from one topic to another without clear boundaries. Over several hours of free-form discussion, most people appear to be more or less just what they are.

5. Dealing with Fraud and Bad Faith

Mediation usually does not work well when the parties are not forthright with the mediator. Some parties have had a history of bad faith negotiations, and bring that history to the mediation. Parties who deny facts that exist, and assert facts that do not exist, may cripple the mediator. The urge to reach for advantage may be curbed in the courtroom when a party is under oath, but there may be no such restraint in a mediation. Sometimes there is so much anger or desire for punishment on one or both sides that objectivity is just not possible. In other cases, one side benefits inordinately from delay. Under these circumstances, mediation will only rarely arrive at a settlement.

Experienced lawyers who see these factors at work worry about spending time on a mediation that cannot succeed.

Page 328. Add at the bottom of the page:

6. Ethical Issues

What ethical constraints should apply to lawyers representing clients in a mediation? Compare Comment [5] under proposed Rule 2.4 of ABA 2000:

> [5] Lawyers who represent clients in alternative dispute-resolution processes are governed by the Rules of Professional Conduct. When the dispute-resolution process takes place before a tribunal, as in binding arbitration (see Rule 1.0(m)) the lawyer's duty of candor is governed by Rule 3.3. Otherwise, the lawyer's duty of candor toward both the third-party neutral and other parties is governed by Rule 4.1.

with Kimberlee Kovach (2001) "New Wine Requires New Wineskins: Transforming Lawyer Ethics for Effective Representation in a Non-Adversarial Approach to Problem Solving: Mediation," 28 *Fordham Urb. L.J.* 935, proposing a "more collaborative and cooperative" set of rules, involving such obligations as good faith or minimum meaningful participation and "an ethic of care." Who has the better approach here? If Professor Kovach, how might you concretely flesh out her goal? What difficulties do you see with her approach?

E. MAKING THE DECISION TO SETTLE: DECISION ANALYSIS

Page 335. Insert the following at the end of text preceding the Questions.

Some Questions About Decision Analysis

If decision analysis is such a useful technique, why is it not used more widely? Undoubtedly some of the explanation lies in the complexity of the process and the

Chapter 5.   Combining and Applying the Basic Process   Page 335

fact that many negotiators and mediators are unfamiliar with it. But surely there is more to it than that.

A primary problem is the delusive sense of precision that is conveyed by the specific numbers that are used in the process. At first glance it seems very persuasive when one concludes, as one moves from right to left on the decision tree, that the plaintiff's case is worth $622,100. But is this a somewhat refined and attenuated example of "garbage in, garbage out"? If the basic numbers that make up the decision tree are essentially the result of educated guesswork, how much confidence can we have in the final number?

There is another problem. Not only do the precise numbers provide a false sense of security; they also omit altogether nonquantifiable factors that may prove to be critical in specific cases. The most obvious of these is risk aversion. Since decision analysis is premised on applying the law of averages to various transactions, a plaintiff who would rather have $800 in hand than a 20 percent chance of getting $5,000 might be easily misled. One way to avoid this result is to stop the decision analysis before taking the final step of creating an "expected value" by summing across the product of each potential outcome multiplied by its likelihood of occurrence. If instead the lawyer presents the various potential outcomes with their accompanying likelihoods (e.g., telling the client she has a 20 percent chance of $5,000 and an 80 percent chance of $0 rather than merely an expected value of $1,000) and allows the client to assess which approach she prefers, the client can take into account her risk aversion in selecting the appropriate approach.

While decision analysis does not purport to evaluate the impact of intangible factors (like fear and anger), those factors may be critical in negotiations or mediations. Consider a medical malpractice case against a pediatric surgeon for negligently causing the death of a musically gifted child. After futile efforts to bridge the monetary gap between the plaintiff and defendant, the mediator sensed that there was more at stake here than money and began to explore ways in which the defendant doctor might address the parents' primary concerns. A solution was worked out involving an expression of sympathy and regret by the doctor, along with an offer to set up a small prize, named after the deceased child, to help other musically gifted children advance their musical training. To avoid situations like this, parties using decision analysis to assist them in negotiations or mediations should remain cognizant that the process may result in positional entrenchment and that efforts should be made to overcome this entrenchment through consideration of non-monetary factors.

So what are the conclusions that can be drawn from this brief examination of the inherent limitations of decision analysis?

1. Don't be deluded by the apparent precision of the technique. Indeed it may be the *process* of constructing a decision tree, and the resulting dialogue that it usually generates between opposing parties, that is more valuable than any end figure,

Page 335   Chapter 5.   Combining and Applying the Basic Process

because that discussion often highlights the key differences between plaintiff and defendant. Once those are identified, additional tools (such as expert opinions) can be utilized.

2. Decision analysis is not a substitute for probing for interests, because, as in the cited medical example, there may be nonmonetary factors that are critical in any specific case.

3. Decision analysis is one flawed but useful tool that must be used with caution and discretion, along with other more traditional dispute resolution techniques.

F. DISPUTE SYSTEMS DESIGN

Page 354.   Immediately before the Questions, insert the following Note:

Two Current Applications of Dispute Systems Design

A. E-ADR

Just as the Internet has revolutionized the transmission of information generally, so it has had a potentially far-reaching impact on the practice of ADR (Katsh and Rifkin, 2001).

There are two types of disputes that are amenable to electronic ADR: (1) disputes that are created by the existence of the Internet (e.g., controversies over domain names or disputes resulting from Internet transactions); and (2) disputes arising out of non-Internet dealings (e.g., a traditional commercial transaction using the Internet to provide dispute resolution services).

Questions

5.27A   As an example of the former category, assume that your client, Internet Commerce (IC), acts as an agent for cyberspace buyers and sellers of merchandise of all kinds who are located all over the world. For a 3 percent commission from the seller on completed sales, IC monitors the quality of merchandise, thus giving the buyer, who generally has no opportunity to inspect the merchandise, some assurance of reliability. This in turn leads buyers to prefer IC-covered products.

IC now comes to you and tells you that it envisions a variety of disputes that may arise from these transactions (e.g., disputes about quality, damaged merchandise, missing items, etc.). It asks you to set up an electronic scheme for effectively handling the envisioned disputes, using the schema set forth on pages 339-348 of the

Chapter 5. Combining and Applying the Basic Process   Page 354

casebook. What will be the key features of such a scheme? What differences in the electronic climate will require special treatment as compared with in-person DR schemes?

B. Streams of Cases*

In a number of situations the legal system is presented by a large number of claims (a stream of cases) requiring efficient, low-transaction-cost resolution (Shaw and Cohn, 1999).

Streams of cases can arise in a variety of contexts: class actions, mass tort situations, and when there are a number of similar claims against a single defendant, as arises often in workplace settings. The subject of streams is often linked with a discussion of hybrids because streams are often dealt with through multi-step procedures or procedures which combine elements of mediation and arbitration.

The need to address streams of cases can arise both pre- and post-dispute.

Pre-dispute: In-house dispute resolution programs
Cases expected to arise out of a natural disaster (e.g., World Trade Center disaster, Hurricane Andrew, Oakland Landslide)
Construction projects

Post-dispute: Class actions (pre- and post-class certification)
Mass torts (e.g., asbestos, Dalkon shield, breast implant litigation)
Bankruptcy (e.g., Drexel Burnham and Milken, Bradlees Stores)

Well-articulated principles of system design are often applied in handling pre-dispute streams (see Goldberg, Brett and Ury, pp. 339-348).

There are some special and unique pressures in designing processes for handling post-dispute streams:

- tension between efficiency/low transaction costs and giving fair consideration to individual claims (i.e., when is "rough justice" not enough justice);
- people designing the system or who must be consulted about the system design are often self-interested; often there are others whose interests must

---

*We are indebted to Margaret Shaw of ADR Associates in New York City for this material and the two Questions that follow. Copyright © Margaret L. Shaw, ADR Associates, LLC, 1350 Broadway, Suite 1350, NYC 10018. Not to be reproduced without written permission.

be taken into account (e.g., class members who are pro se or represented by independent counsel);
- in some situations (e.g., class actions) the system must be designed without knowing the number of claims;
- in other types of cases (e.g., asbestos) the question is how future claims will be addressed (how much, if anything, should be reserved for future claims);
- claimants and/or counsel may be geographically dispersed;
- repeat player issues (between attorneys, between neutrals and attorneys); and
- the extent to which individual settlements and awards should be consistent.

Consider the following two problems:

5.27B The EEOC brought suit against Astra USA, Inc., a pharmaceutical company, alleging, inter alia, claims of hostile work environment and retaliation under Title VII of the Civil Rights Act. The suit alleged widespread sexual harassment throughout the company, including by the company's top management. Individual claims varied, and included a range of behavior from repetitive incidents of touching to offensive statements to pressure to sign a letter disavowing knowledge of harassment at the company.

The suit was settled, and the Consent Decree provided for the establishment of a Claim Fund in the amount of $9.9 million to be distributed by a special master appointed by the court pursuant to Rule 53 of the Federal Rules of Civil Procedure.

One hundred eighty-three claim forms detailing each claimant's allegations and damages were received by the special master. How should she go about distributing the Claim Fund?

5.27C Your law firm is contemplating filing a class action against Investment Advisers (IA), a large company with offices all around the country. The conduct complained of includes a variety of race discrimination claims (e.g., failure to promote, salary differentials and hostile environment). The parties decided to mediate at the pre-class-certification stage. There are six named plaintiffs, who have raised both state and federal claims.

The potential class could involve current as well as former employees; the parties' estimates of the class size vary wildly from about 100 on the one hand to as many as 550 on the other. All plaintiffs will be represented by the same law firm.

While the parties, in theory, are all interested in an expeditious process, the plaintiffs are concerned about the company's perceived power; they want to make sure the company "gets it" in terms of race issues in their workplace, and they also want current employees to have the opportunity to resolve their claims quickly if they so desire and be able to move on. The company is very concerned about

Chapter 5. Combining and Applying the Basic Process

discouraging unmeritorious claims, and also wants to protect their local managers from being pilloried in the press.

What kind of claims resolution process would you recommend for handling this case? Would you recommend a fixed fund or no fixed fund? A cap on the amount of settlement or award for any individual claimant or no cap? An adversarial or settlement-oriented process? Any aggregation of claims? What type of relief would be recoverable? Who would pay attorneys' fees? How would the process you recommend be administered? What would be the bases for your recommendation? What would be the major objections to your recommendation that would likely be raised? How would you respond?

Page 357. Add to the References:

KATSH, Ethan, and Janet RIFKIN (2001) *Online Dispute Resolution.* San Francisco: Jossey-Bass.

SHAW, Margaret, and Lynn COHN (1999) "Employment Class Action Settlements Provide Unique Context for ADR," *Dis. Res. Mag.* 10 (Summer).

SYMPOSIUM (2000) "ADR in Cyberspace," 15 *Ohio St. J. Dis. Res.*, No. 3.

6
COURTS AND ADR

Page 403. Add to Question 6.14:

In 2001 the National Conference of Commissioners on Uniform State Laws weighed in on this debate. The Uniform Mediation Act prohibits mediator recommendations of the type criticized by Professor Grillo. Read Section 7 of the Act (Appendix J). Assuming that a court requires the parties to engage in good faith negotiation (see casebook pp. 399-401), what are the advantages and disadvantages of permitting a mediator to tell the judge that the parties did or did not negotiate in good faith?

7
CONFIDENTIALITY

Page 430. **Add the following case and discussion at the bottom of the page (after Question 7.10).**

Accommodating the Interests of Justice: Predictability Versus Fine Tuning

If the *Castellano* (casebook p. 428) mediation took place today, the pertinent Florida mediation privilege statute would not authorize the court to enforce the subpoena. Defense counsel would be left with the argument that the criminal defendant's constitutional rights require the privilege to yield (see *Davis v. Alaska*, 415 U.S. 308 (1974) (confidentiality of juvenile record must yield to a criminal defendant's rights to confront witnesses)).

Of course, a state could deal with the compelling need for evidence in criminal cases like *Castellano* by enacting a mediation privilege that is applicable only to civil proceedings. California did just that. In the case below, U.S. Magistrate Judge Wayne Brazil (a supporter of mediation and author of the article on casebook p. 404) considers whether a statutory mediation privilege should yield to a strong need for evidence even in a civil case.

OLAM v. CONGRESS MORTGAGE COMPANY
68 F. Supp. 2d 1110 (N.D. Cal. 1999)

WAYNE D. BRAZIL, UNITED STATES MAGISTRATE JUDGE

The court addresses in this opinion several difficult issues about the relationship between a court-sponsored voluntary mediation and subsequent proceedings whose purpose is to determine whether the parties entered an enforceable agreement at the close of the mediation session.

As we explain below, . . . the parties participated in a lengthy mediation [of a case involving the federal Truth in Lending Act and related state and federal claims] that was hosted by this court's ADR Program Counsel [, Mr. Herman] — an employee of the court who is both a lawyer and an ADR professional. At the end of the mediation (after midnight), the parties signed a "Memorandum of Understanding"

47

(MOU) that states that it is "intended as a binding document itself...." Contending that the consent she apparently gave was not legally valid, plaintiff [, Mrs. Olam,] has taken the position that the MOU is not enforceable. She has not complied with its terms. Defendants have filed a motion to enforce the MOU as a binding contract.

One of the principal issues with which the court wrestles, below, is whether evidence about what occurred during the mediation proceedings, including testimony from the mediator, may be used to help resolve this dispute....

[WHAT LAW APPLIES TO THE USE OF EVIDENCE FROM THE MEDIATION]

Counsel for plaintiff [, Mrs. Olam,] contended that the parties must be presumed ... to have entered the mediation process expecting federal law to serve as the source of the protection of the confidentiality of the mediation proceedings. Plaintiff further argued that such expectations were reasonable and that it would be unfair not to honor them.

In support of that contention, plaintiff emphasized that the mediation took place expressly under the auspices of this court's ADR program—and that there has been in effect in this court for a good many years a local rule that purports to fix the terms under which mediation confidences will be protected....

The core problem in plaintiff's approach is that it ignores the express provision of Federal Rule of Evidence 501 that appears to be applicable here. That provision ... directs that "in civil actions and proceedings, with respect to an element of a claim or defense as to which State law supplies the rule of decision, the privilege of a witness ... shall be determined in accordance with State law." Defendants' motion to enforce the settlement agreement is a civil proceeding in which state law, and only state law, provides the rule of decision. The only question that motion raises is whether the parties entered an enforceable contract at the conclusion of the mediation—and the rule of decision for resolving this one substantive question will have only one source—the substantive law of the state of California.

Given these undisputed and foreseeable circumstances, the parties should have understood, before their mediation, that if, later, one party initiated proceedings designed to secure a determination that the mediation produced an enforceable settlement contract disputes about the confidentiality of mediation communications would be resolved in those proceedings by applying the law of the state of California....

[WHO HOLDS THE PRIVILEGE]

California law confers on mediators a privilege that is independent of the privilege conferred on parties to a mediation. By declaring that, subject to exceptions

Chapter 7. Confidentiality — Page 430

not applicable here, mediators are incompetent to testify "as to any statement, conduct, decision, or ruling, occurring at or in conjunction with [the mediation]," section 703.5 of the Evidence Code has the effect of making a mediator the holder of an independent privilege. Section 1119 of the Evidence Code appears to have the same effect—as it prohibits courts from compelling disclosure of evidence about mediation communications and directs that all such communications "shall remain confidential." As the California Court of Appeal recently pointed out, "the Legislature intended that the confidentiality provision of section 1119 may be asserted by the mediator as well as by the participants in the mediation." It follows that, under California law, a waiver of the mediation privilege by the parties is not a sufficient basis for a court to permit or order a mediator to testify. Rather, an independent determination must be made before testimony from a mediator should be permitted or ordered. . . .

[T]he court announced that it would proceed on the assumption that Mr. Herman [, the mediator,] was respectfully and appropriately asserting the mediator's privilege and was formally objecting to being called to testify about anything said or done during the mediation. . . .

[WEIGHING THE NEED FOR EVIDENCE AND THE INTEREST IN PROTECTING CONFIDENTIALITY]

In [Rinaker v. Superior Court, 62 Cal. App. 4th 155 (3d Dist. 1998),] the Court of Appeal held that there may be circumstances in which a trial court, over vigorous objection by a party and by the mediator, could compel testimony from the mediator in a juvenile delinquency proceeding [deemed a "civil" matter under California law]. The defendant in the delinquency proceeding wanted to call the mediator to try to impeach testimony that was expected from a prosecution witness. That witness and the delinquency defendant had earlier participated in a mediation—and the delinquency defendant believed that the complaining witness had made admissions to the mediator that would substantially undermine the credibility of the complaining witnesses' testimony—and thus would materially strengthen the defense. In these circumstances, the *Rinaker* court held that the mediator could be compelled to testify if, after in camera consideration of what her testimony would be, the trial judge determined that her testimony might well promote significantly the public interest in preventing perjury and the defendant's fundamental right to a fair judicial process. . . .

[T]he court is to weigh and comparatively assess (1) the importance of the values and interests that would be harmed if the mediator was compelled to testify (perhaps subject to a sealing or protective order, if appropriate), (2) the magnitude of the harm that compelling the testimony would cause to those values and interests, (3) the importance of the rights or interests that would be jeopardized if the mediator's

49

testimony was not accessible in the specific proceedings in question, and (4) how much the testimony would contribute toward protecting those rights or advancing those interests—an inquiry that includes, among other things, an assessment of whether there are alternative sources of evidence of comparable probative value. . . .

Like many other variables in this kind of analysis, however, the magnitude of these risks can vary with the circumstances. Here, for instance, all parties to the mediation want the mediator to testify about things that occurred during the mediation—so ordering the testimony would do less harm to the actual relationships developed than it would in a case where one of the parties to the mediation objected. . . .

We acknowledge, however, that the possibility that a mediator might be forced to testify over objection could harm the capacity of mediators in general to create the environment of trust that they feel maximized the likelihood that constructive communication will occur during the mediation session. But the level of harm to that interest likely varies, at least in some measure, with the perception within the community of mediators and litigants about how likely it is that any given mediation will be followed at some point by an order compelling the neutral to offer evidence about what occurred during the session. . . . [T]his case represents the first time that I have been called upon to address these kinds of questions in the more than fifteen years that I have been responsible for ADR programs in this court. Nor am I aware of the issue arising before other judges here. Based on that experience, my partially educated guess is that the likelihood that a mediator or the parties in any given case need fear that the mediator would later be constrained to testify is extraordinarily small.

That conviction is reinforced by another consideration. As we pointed out above, under California law, and this court's view of sound public policy, there should be no occasion to consider whether to seek testimony from a mediator for [the] purpose of determining whether the parties entered an enforceable settlement contract unless the mediation produced a writing (or competent record) that appears on its face to constitute an enforceable contract, signed or formally assented to by all the parties. Thus, it is only when there is such a writing or record, and when a party nonetheless seeks to escape its apparent effect, that courts applying California law would even consider calling for evidence from a mediator for purposes of determining whether the parties settled the case. Surely these circumstances will arise after only a tiny fraction of mediations.

The magnitude of the risk to values underlying the mediation privilege . . . that can be created by ordering a mediator to testify also can vary with the nature of the testimony that is sought. . . .

[T]he kind of testimony sought from the mediator in this case poses less of a threat to fairness and reliability values than the kind of testimony that was sought from the mediator in *Rinaker*. During the first stage balancing analysis in the case at bar, the parties and I assumed that the testimony from the mediator that would be most consequential would focus not primarily on what Ms. Olam said during the mediation, but on how she acted and the mediator's perceptions of her physical, emotional, and mental condition. The purpose would not be to nail down and dissect her specific words, but to assess at a more general and impressionistic level her condition and capacities. That purpose might be achieved with relatively little disclosure of the content of her confidential communications. . . .

The interests that are likely to be advanced by compelling the mediator to testify in this case are of considerable importance. . . .

The first interest we identify is the interest in doing justice. For reasons described below, the mediator is positioned in this case to offer what could be crucial, certainly very probative, evidence about the central factual issues in this matter. . . .

In sharp contrast, refusing to compel the mediator to testify might well deprive the court of the evidence it needs to rule reliably on the plaintiff's contentions—and thus might either cause the court to impose an unjust outcome on the plaintiff or disable the court from enforcing the settlement. In this setting, refusing to compel testimony from the mediator that may address its condition and capacities might end up being tantamount to denying the motion to enforce the agreement—because a crucial source of evidence about the plaintiff's condition and capacities would be missing. Following that course, defendants suggest, would do considerable harm not only to the court's mediation program but also to fundamental fairness. If parties believed that courts routinely would refuse to compel mediators to testify, and that the absence of evidence from mediators would enhance the viability of a contention that apparent consent to a settlement contract was not legally viable, cynical parties would be encouraged either to try to escape commitments they made during mediations or to use threats of such escapes to try to renegotiate, after the mediation, more favorable terms—terms that they never would have been able to secure without this artificial and unfair leverage. . . .

[ENFORCEABILITY OF THE MEMORANDUM
OF UNDERSTANDING]

[The court reviews the evidence, including the mediator's testimony, and concludes:] Because plaintiff has failed to prove either of the necessary elements of undue influence, and because she has established no other grounds to escape the contract she signed on September 10, 1998, the court grants defendants' Motion to Enforce the settlement contract that is memorialized in the MOU.

Note on "Qualified" v. "Categorical" Privilege

If one likes Judge Brazil's balancing approach, a logical statutory approach would be to propose a "qualified" mediation privilege statute that specifically authorizes the court to do what Judge Brazil did in *Olam*—to weigh the need for evidence in the individual case against the purposes served by the privilege (see Ohio Rev. Code §2317.023). A disadvantage of a qualified privilege is the parties' inability, at the time of mediation, to predict the need for evidence, and therefore whether their statements at the mediation will be admitted into evidence. Another statutory option is a "categorical" approach in which the privilege is stated in absolute terms but the statute sets out a series of exceptions that reflect an a priori weighing of confidentiality versus the likely need for evidence of this type. The categorical approach permits the parties to gauge the breadth of confidentiality at the time of the mediation, at least to the extent that the exceptions yield clear results. Even these exceptions do not improve predictability, however, if they depend on the use made later of the evidence, such as whether it is offered in a child protection proceeding, or if they depend in part on the need for the evidence. In 2001 the National Conference of Commissioners on Uniform State Laws, the group that drafted the Uniform Commercial Code, approved a Uniform Mediation Act (Appendix J), which takes a "categorical" approach for the most part. The Act contains nine exceptions. However, the drafters could not resist introducing a balancing test for two of the exceptions. In addition, some exceptions apply only in some kinds of proceedings. Had the Act been applicable to the mediation in *Olam*, the pertinent provisions would have been the following:

UNIFORM MEDIATION ACT

SECTION 6. EXCEPTIONS TO PRIVILEGE.

(b) There is no privilege under Section 4 if a court, administrative agency, or arbitrator finds, after a hearing in camera, that the party seeking discovery or the proponent of the evidence has shown that the evidence is not otherwise available, that there is a need for the evidence that substantially outweighs the interest in protecting confidentiality, and that the mediation communication is sought or offered in: . . .

  (2) except as otherwise provided in subsection (c), a proceeding to prove a claim to rescind or reform or a defense to avoid liability on a contract arising out of the mediation.

  (c) A mediator may not be compelled to provide evidence of a mediation communication referred to in subsection . . . (b)(2). . . .

Were the Uniform Law Commissioners right to exempt the mediator from testifying?

Chapter 7. Confidentiality Page 430

Conflict of Laws

The Uniform Mediation Act also responds to another issue raised by the *Olam* case: certainty at the time of the mediation about what jurisdiction's privilege law will apply to mediation. In *Olam,* one party claimed surprise that the privilege for a federal court mediation would be governed by California law, especially when some of the substantive claims in the case were based in federal law. The Uniform Mediation Act (see Appendix J), if widely adopted by the states, deals with a comparable problem across state jurisdictions. The Reporter's Notes explain:

> Uniformity of the law helps bring order and understanding across state lines, and encourages effective use of mediation in a number of ways. First, uniformity is a necessary predicate to predictability if there is any potential that a statement made in mediation in one State may be sought in litigation or other legal processes in another State. Without uniformity, there can be no firm assurance in any State that a mediation is privileged.
>
> A second benefit of uniformity relates to cross-jurisdictional mediation. Mediation sessions are increasingly conducted by conference calls between mediators and parties in different States and even over the Internet. Because it is unclear which State's laws apply, the parties cannot be assured of the reach of their home state's confidentiality protections.
>
> A third benefit of uniformity is that a party trying to decide whether to sign an agreement to mediate may not know where the mediation will occur and therefore whether the law will provide a privilege or the right to bring counsel or support person. Uniformity will add certainty on these issues, and thus allows for more informed party self-determination.
>
> Finally, uniformity contributes to simplicity. Mediators and parties who do not have meaningful familiarity with the law or legal research currently face a more formidable task in understanding multiple confidentiality statutes that vary by and within relevant States than they would in understanding a Uniform Act. Mediators and parties often travel to different States for the mediation sessions. If they do not understand these legal protections, participants may react in a guarded way, thus reducing the candor that these provisions are designed to promote, or they may unnecessarily expend resources to have the legal research conducted.

Questions

7.10.1 What is gained by the Uniform Mediation Act (Appendix J) in terms of the parties' ability to predict whether their mediation discussions will be used in legal proceedings? How would you suggest changing the Act to enhance predictability?

Would it be better if the Act just authorized the courts to weigh the interests (confidentiality versus need for evidence) in each case, as Judge Brazil did in *Olam*?

7.10.2 Review Section 8 of the Uniform Mediation Act (Appendix J). What would be gained and lost if the Act prohibited disclosure of mediation communications outside of legal proceedings (e.g., discussions with friends)?

7.10.3 Judge Brazil has referred your client's federal claim to mediation before the federal district court mediator. The federal court local rule simply prohibits use of mediation communications in any court proceeding. If California has enacted the Uniform Mediation Act (Appendix J), what advice should you give to your client about the extent of confidentiality for that session?

7.10.4 A bill containing the Uniform Mediation Act (Appendix J) has been introduced in your state legislature. What would be gained or lost if your state modified the Act to make the parties the only holders of the privilege?

7.10.5 Under the Uniform Mediation Act, what protection does a mediation party have if another participant makes important false statements?

8
FAMILY DISPUTES

Page 472. Add the following to question 8.1:

Interestingly, the new Model Standards of Practice for Family and Divorce Mediation (Appendix I) do not address the question of whether mediators should be authorized to or prohibited from excluding lawyers from a mediation session. The National Conference of Commissioners on Uniform State Laws, by contrast, came down on the side of the lawyer-participation approach advocated by Professors McEwen and Rogers (casebook pp. 407-409) in approving the Uniform Mediation Act. Read Section 10 of the Act (Appendix J). What are the arguments for and against enactment of this section of the Act by the states?

9
PUBLIC DISPUTES

Page 492. **Before the Questions, insert:**

An important new book for resolving public disputes is Lawrence Susskind, Sarah McKearnan, and Jennifer Thomas-Larner, eds. (1999) *Consensus Building Handbook.* Thousand Oaks, Ca.: Sage (17 chapters on all aspects of consensus-based resolutions along with 17 illustrative annotated case studies).

10
INTERNATIONAL DISPUTES

Page 555. **Add the following reference before the Brett article:**

See Brett (2001) *Negotiating Globally*. San Francisco: Jossey-Bass.

11
THE FUTURE OF ADR

Page 572. **Add the following before the Questions:**

The Texas legislature is apparently the first legislative body to recognize collaborative lawyering in family dissolution and parent-child proceedings. See Texas Family Code §§6.603, 153.0072 (2001).

Appendix H
REVISED UNIFORM ARBITRATION ACT (2000)[*]

[The blackletter text and explanatory notes for the RUAA may be found by entering the following address: *http://www.law.upenn.edu/bll/ulc/ulc_frame.htm* and clicking on the appropriate links at the site].

PREFATORY NOTE

The Uniform Arbitration Act (UAA), promulgated in 1955, has been one of the most successful Acts of the National Conference of Commissioners on Uniform State Laws. Forty-nine jurisdictions have arbitration statutes; 35 of these have adopted the UAA and 14 have adopted substantially similar legislation. A primary purpose of the 1955 Act was to insure the enforceability of agreements to arbitrate in the face of oftentimes hostile state law. That goal has been accomplished. Today arbitration is a primary mechanism favored by courts and parties to resolve disputes in many areas of the law. This growth in arbitration caused the Conference to appoint a Drafting Committee to consider revising the Act in light of the increasing use of arbitration, the greater complexity of many disputes resolved by arbitration, and the developments of the law in this area.

The UAA did not address many issues which arise in modern arbitration cases. The statute provided no guidance as to (1) who decides the arbitrability of a dispute and by what criteria; (2) whether a court or arbitrators may issue provisional remedies; (3) how a party can initiate an arbitration proceeding; (4) whether arbitration proceedings may be consolidated; (5) whether arbitrators are required to disclose facts reasonably likely to affect impartiality; (6) what extent arbitrators or an arbitration organization are immune from civil actions; (7) whether arbitrators or representatives of arbitration organizations may be required to testify in another proceeding; (8) whether arbitrators have the discretion to order discovery, issue protective orders, decide motions for summary dispositions, hold prehearing conferences and otherwise manage the arbitration process; (9) when a court may enforce

---

[*] © 2000 by the National Conference of Commissioners on Uniform State Laws. Reprinted with permission.

a preaward ruling by an arbitrator; (10) what remedies an arbitrator may award, especially in regard to attorney's fees, punitive damages or other exemplary relief; (11) when a court can award attorney's fees and costs to arbitrators and arbitration organizations; (12) when a court can award attorney's fees and costs to a prevailing party in an appeal of an arbitrator's award; and (13) which sections of the UAA would not be waivable, an important matter to insure fundamental fairness to the parties will be preserved, particularly in those instances where one party may have significantly less bargaining power than another; and (14) the use of electronic information and other modern means of technology in the arbitration process. The Revised Uniform Arbitration Act (RUAA) examines all of these issues and provides state legislatures with a more up-to-date statute to resolve disputes through arbitration.

There are a number of principles that the Drafting Committee agreed upon at the outset of its consideration of a revision to the UAA. First, arbitration is a consensual process in which autonomy of the parties who enter into arbitration agreements should be given primary consideration, so long as their agreements conform to notions of fundamental fairness. This approach provides parties with the opportunity in most instances to shape the arbitration process to their own particular needs. In most instances the RUAA provides a default mechanism if the parties do not have a specific agreement on a particular issue. Second, the underlying reason many parties choose arbitration is the relative speed, lower cost, and greater efficiency of the process. The law should take these factors, where applicable, into account. For example, Section 10 allows consolidation of issues involving multiple parties. Such a provision can be of special importance in adhesion situations where there are numerous persons with essentially the same claims against a party to the arbitration agreement. Finally, in most cases parties intend the decisions of arbitrators to be final with minimal court involvement unless there is clear unfairness or a denial of justice. This contractual nature of arbitration means that the provision to vacate awards in Section 23 is limited. This is so even where an arbitrator may award attorney's fees, punitive damages or other exemplary relief under Section 21. Section 14 insulates arbitrators from unwarranted litigation to insure their independence by providing them with immunity.

Other new provisions are intended to reflect developments in arbitration law and to insure that the process is a fair one. Section 12 requires arbitrators to make important disclosures to the parties. Section 8 allows courts to grant provisional remedies in certain circumstances to protect the integrity of the arbitration process. Section 17 includes limited rights to discovery while recognizing the importance of expeditious arbitration proceedings.

In light of a number of decisions by the United States Supreme Court concerning the Federal Arbitration Act (FAA), any revision of the UAA must take into account the doctrine of preemption. The rule of preemption, whereby FAA standards and the emphatically pro-arbitration perspective of the FAA control, applies in both the federal courts and the state courts. To date, the preemption-related opinions of the Supreme Court have centered in large part on the two key issues that arise at the front end of the arbitration process—enforcement of the agreement to arbitrate and issues of substantive arbitrability. *Prima Paint Corp. v. Flood & Conklin Mfg. Co.*, 388 U.S. 35 (1967); *Moses H. Cone Mem'l Hosp. v. Mercury Constr. Corp.*, 460 U.S. 1 (1983); *Southland Corp. v. Keating*, 465 U.S. 2 (1984); *Perry v. Thomas*, 482 U.S. 483 (1987); *Allied-Bruce Terminix Cos. v. Dobson*, 513 U.S. 265 (1995); *Doctor's Assocs. v. Cassarotto*, 517 U.S. 681 (1996). That body of case law establishes that state law of any ilk, including adaptations of the RUAA, mooting or limiting contractual agreements to arbitrate must yield to the pro-arbitration public policy voiced in Sections 2, 3, and 4 of the FAA.

The other issues to which the FAA speaks definitively lie at the back end of the arbitration process. The standards and procedure for vacatur, confirmation and modification of arbitration awards are the subject of Sections 9, 10, 11, and 12 of the FAA. In contrast to the "front end" issues of enforceability and substantive arbitrability, there is no definitive Supreme Court case law speaking to the preemptive effect, if any, of the FAA with regard to these "back end" issues. This dimension of FAA preemption of state arbitration law is further complicated by the strong majority view among the United States Circuit Courts of Appeals that the Section 10(a) standards are not the exclusive grounds for vacatur.

Nevertheless, the Supreme Court's unequivocal stand to date as to the preemptive effect of the FAA provides strong reason to believe that a similar result will obtain with regard to Section 10(a) grounds for vacatur. If it does, and if the Supreme Court eventually determines that the Section 10(a) standards are the sole grounds for vacatur of commercial arbitration awards, FAA preemption of conflicting state law with regard to the "back end" issues of vacatur (and confirmation and modification) would be certain. If the Court takes the opposite tack and holds that the Section 10(a) grounds are not the exclusive criteria for vacatur, the preemptive effect of Section 10(a) would most likely be limited to the rule that state arbitration acts cannot eliminate, limit or modify any of the four grounds of party and arbitrator misconduct set out in Section 10(a). Any definitive federal "common law," pertaining to the nonstatutory grounds for vacatur other than those set out in Section 10(a), articulated by the Supreme Court or established as a clear majority rule by the United States Courts of Appeals, likely would preempt contrary state law. A holding by the Supreme Court that the Section 10(a) grounds are not exclusive would also free the States to codify other grounds for vacatur beyond those set out in Section 10(a). These various, currently nonstatutory grounds for vacatur are discussed at length in Section C to the Comment to Section 23.

An important caveat to the general rule of FAA preemption is found in *Volt Information Sciences, Inc. v. Stanford University*, 489 U.S. 468 (1989) and *Mastrobuono v. Shearson Lehman Hutton, Inc.*, 514 U.S. 52 (1995). The focus in these cases is on the effect of FAA preemption on choice-of-law provisions routinely included in commercial contracts. *Volt* and *Mastrobuono* establish that a clearly expressed contractual agreement by the parties to an arbitration contract to conduct their arbitration under state law rules effectively trumps the preemptive effect of the FAA. If the parties elect to govern their contractual arbitration mechanism by the law of a particular State and thereby limit the issues that they will arbitrate or the procedures under which the arbitration will be conducted, their bargain will be honored—as long as the state law principles invoked by the choice-of-law provision do not conflict with the FAA's prime directive that agreements to arbitrate be enforced. *See, e.g., ASW Allstate Painting & Constr. Co. v. Lexington Ins. Co.*, 188 F.3d 307 (5th Cir. 1999); *Russ Berrie & Co. v. Gantt*, 988 S.W.2d 713 (Tex. Ct. App. 1999). It is in these situations that the RUAA will have most impact. Section 4(a) of the RUAA also explicitly provides that the parties to an arbitration agreement may waive or vary the terms of the Act to the extent otherwise permitted by law. Thus, when parties choose to contractually specify the procedures to be followed under their arbitration agreement, the RUAA contemplates that the contractually-established procedures will control over contrary state law, except with regard to issues designated as "nonwaivable" in Section 4(b) and (c) of the RUAA.

The contractual election to proceed under state law instead of the FAA will be honored presuming that the state law is not antithetical to the pro-arbitration public policy of the FAA. *Southland* and *Terminix* leave no doubt that anti-arbitration state law provisions will be struck down because preempted by the federal arbitration statute.

Besides arbitration contracts where the parties choose to be governed by state law, there are other areas of arbitration law where the FAA does not preempt state law, in the absence of definitive federal law set out in the FAA or determined by the federal courts. First, the Supreme Court has made clear its belief that ascertaining when a particular contractual agreement to arbitrate is enforceable is a matter to be decided under the general contract law principles of each State. The sole limitation on state law in that regard is the Court's assertion that the enforceability of arbitration agreements must be determined by the same standards as are used for all other contracts. *Terminix*, 513 U.S. at 281 (1995) (quoting *Volt*, 489 U.S. at 474 (1989)) and quoted in *Cassarotto*, 517 U.S. 681, 685 (1996); and *Cassarotto*, 517 U.S. at 688 (quoting *Scherk v. Alberto-Culver Co.*, 417 U.S. 506, 511 (1974)). Arbitration agreements may not be invalidated under state laws applicable only to arbitration provisions. *Id.* The FAA will preempt state law that does not place arbitration agreements on an "equal footing" with other contracts.

During the course of its deliberations the Drafting Committee considered at length another issue with strong preemption undertones—the question of whether the RUAA should explicitly sanction contractual provisions for "opt-in" review of challenged arbitration awards beyond that presently contemplated by the FAA and current state arbitration acts. "Opt-in" provisions of two types are in limited use today. The first variant permits a party who is dissatisfied with the arbitral result to petition directly to a designated state court and stipulates that the court may vacate challenged awards, typically for errors of law or fact. The second type of "opt-in" contractual provision establishes an appellate arbitral mechanism to which challenged arbitration awards can be submitted for review, again most typically for errors of law or fact.

As explained in detail in Section B of the Comment to Section 23, there were a number of reasons that resulted in the decision not to include statutory sanction of the "opt-in" device for expanded judicial review in the RUAA: (1) the current uncertainty as to the legality of a state statutory sanction of the "opt-in" device, (2) the "disconnect" between the Act's purpose of fostering the use of arbitration as a final and binding alternative to traditional litigation in a court of law, and (3) the inclusion of a statutory provision that would permit the parties to contractually render arbitration decidedly non-final and non-binding. Simply stated, the potential gain to be realized by codifying a right to opt-into expanded judicial review that has not yet been definitively confirmed to exist does not outweigh the potential threat that adoption of an opt-in statutory provision would create for the integrity and viability of the RUAA as a template for state arbitration acts.

Unlike the "opt-in" judicial review mechanism, there are few, if any, legal concerns raised by statutory sanction of "opt-in" provisions for appellate arbitral review. Nevertheless, as explained in the Section B of the Comments to Section 23, because the current, contract-based view of arbitration establishes that the parties are free to design the inner workings of their arbitration procedures in any manner they see fit, the Drafting Committee determined that codification of that right in the RUAA would add nothing of substance to the existing law of arbitration.

The decision not to statutorily sanction either form of the "opt-in" device in the RUAA leaves the issue of the legal propriety of this means for securing review of awards to the developing case law under the FAA and state arbitration statutes. Parties remain free, within the constraints imposed by the existing and developing law, to agree to contractual provisions for arbitral or judicial review of challenged awards.

It is likely that matters not addressed in the FAA are also open to regulation by the States. State law provisions regulating purely procedural dimensions of the arbitration process (*e.g.*, discovery [RUAA Section 17], consolidation of claims [RUAA Section 10], and arbitrator immunity [RUAA Section 14]) likely will not be subject to preemption. Less certain is the effect of FAA preemption with regard to substantive issues like the authority of arbitrators to award punitive damages (RUAA Section 21) and the standards for arbitrator disclosure of potential conflicts of interest (RUAA Section 12) that have a significant impact on the integrity and/or the adequacy of the arbitration process. These "borderline" issues are not purely procedural in nature but unlike the "front end" and "back end" issues they do not go to the essence of the agreement to arbitrate or effectuation of the arbitral result. Although there is no concrete guidance in the case law, preemption of state law dealing with such matters seems unlikely as long as it cannot be characterized as anti-arbitration or as intended to limit the enforceability or viability of agreements to arbitrate. . . .

SECTION 1. DEFINITIONS.

In This [Act]:

(1) "Arbitration organization" means an association, agency, board, commission, or other entity that is neutral and initiates, sponsors, or administers an arbitration proceeding or is involved in the appointment of an arbitrator.

(2) "Arbitrator" means an individual appointed to render an award, alone or with others, in a controversy that is subject to an agreement to arbitrate.

(3) "Court" means [a court of competent jurisdiction in this State].

(4) "Knowledge" means actual knowledge.

(5) "Person" means an individual, corporation, business trust, estate, trust, partnership, limited liability company, association, joint venture, government; governmental subdivision, agency, or instrumentality; public corporation; or any other legal or commercial entity.

(6) "Record" means information that is inscribed on a tangible medium or that is stored in an electronic or other medium and is retrievable in perceivable form.

SECTION 2. NOTICE.

(a) Except as otherwise provided in this [Act], a person gives notice to another person by taking action that is reasonably necessary to inform the other person in ordinary course, whether or not the other person acquires knowledge of the notice.

(b) A person has notice if the person has knowledge of the notice or has received notice.

(c) A person receives notice when it comes to the person's attention or the notice is delivered at the person's place of residence or place of business, or at another location held out by the person as a place of delivery of such communications.

SECTION 3. WHEN [ACT] APPLIES.

(a) This [Act] governs an agreement to arbitrate made on or after [the effective date of this [Act]].

(b) This [Act] governs an agreement to arbitrate made before [the effective date of this [Act]] if all the parties to the agreement or to the arbitration proceeding so agree in a record.

(c) On or after [a delayed date], this [Act] governs an agreement to arbitrate whenever made.

SECTION 4. EFFECT OF AGREEMENT TO ARBITRATE; NONWAIVABLE PROVISIONS.

(a) Except as otherwise provided in subsections (b) and (c), a party to an agreement to arbitrate or to an arbitration proceeding may waive, or the parties may vary the effect of, the requirements of this [Act] to the extent permitted by law.

(b) Before a controversy arises that is subject to an agreement to arbitrate, a party to the agreement may not:

(1) waive or agree to vary the effect of the requirements of Section 5(a), 6(a), 8, 17(a), 17(b), 26, or 28;

(2) agree to unreasonably restrict the right under Section 9 to notice of the initiation of an arbitration proceeding;

(3) agree to unreasonably restrict the right under Section 12 to disclosure of any facts by a neutral arbitrator; or

(4) waive the right under Section 16 of a party to an agreement to arbitrate to be represented by a lawyer at any proceeding or hearing under this [Act], but an employer and a labor organization may waive the right to representation by a lawyer in a labor arbitration.

(c) A party to an agreement to arbitrate or arbitration proceeding may not waive, or the parties may not vary the effect of, the requirements of this section or Section 3(a), (c), 7, 14, 18, 20(c) or (d), 22, 23, 24, 25(a) or (b), 29, 30, 31, or 32.

SECTION 5. [APPLICATION] FOR JUDICIAL RELIEF.

(a) Except as otherwise provided in Section 28, an [application] for judicial relief under this [Act] must be made by [motion] to the court and heard in the manner provided by law or rule of court for making and hearing [motions].

(b) Unless a civil action involving the agreement to arbitrate is pending, notice of an initial [motion] to the court under this [Act] must be served in the manner provided by law for the service of a summons in a civil action. Otherwise, notice of the motion must be given in the manner provided by law or rule of court for serving [motions] in pending cases.

SECTION 6. VALIDITY OF AGREEMENT TO ARBITRATE.

(a) An agreement contained in a record to submit to arbitration any existing or subsequent controversy arising between the parties to the agreement is valid, enforceable, and irrevocable except upon a ground that exists at law or in equity for the revocation of a contract.

(b) The court shall decide whether an agreement to arbitrate exists or a controversy is subject to an agreement to arbitrate.

(c) An arbitrator shall decide whether a condition precedent to arbitrability has been fulfilled and whether a contract containing a valid agreement to arbitrate is enforceable.

(d) If a party to a judicial proceeding challenges the existence of, or claims that a controversy is not subject to, an agreement to arbitrate, the arbitration proceeding may continue pending final resolution of the issue by the court, unless the court otherwise orders.

Section 7. [Motion] to Compel or Stay Arbitration.

(a) On [motion] of a person showing an agreement to arbitrate and alleging another person's refusal to arbitrate pursuant to the agreement:

(1) if the refusing party does not appear or does not oppose the [motion], the court shall order the parties to arbitrate; and

(2) if the refusing party opposes the [motion], the court shall proceed summarily to decide the issue and order the parties to arbitrate unless it finds that there is no enforceable agreement to arbitrate.

(b) On [motion] of a person alleging that an arbitration proceeding has been initiated or threatened but that there is no agreement to arbitrate, the court shall proceed summarily to decide the issue. If the court finds that there is an enforceable agreement to arbitrate, it shall order the parties to arbitrate.

(c) If the court finds that there is no enforceable agreement, it may not pursuant to subsection (a) or (b) order the parties to arbitrate.

(d) The court may not refuse to order arbitration because the claim subject to arbitration lacks merit or grounds for the claim have not been established.

(e) If a proceeding involving a claim referable to arbitration under an alleged agreement to arbitrate is pending in court, a [motion] under this section must be made in that court. Otherwise a [motion] under this section may be made in any court as provided in Section 27.

(f) If a party makes a [motion] to the court to order arbitration, the court on just terms shall stay any judicial proceeding that involves a claim alleged to be subject to the arbitration until the court renders a final decision under this section.

(g) If the court orders arbitration, the court on just terms shall stay any judicial proceeding that involves a claim subject to the arbitration. If a claim subject to the arbitration is severable, the court may limit the stay to that claim.

Section 8. Provisional Remedies.

(a) Before an arbitrator is appointed and is authorized and able to act, the court, upon [motion] of a party to an arbitration proceeding and for good cause shown, may enter an order for provisional remedies to protect the effectiveness of the arbitration proceeding to the same extent and under the same conditions as if the controversy were the subject of a civil action.

(b) After an arbitrator is appointed and is authorized and able to act:

(1) the arbitrator may issue such orders for provisional remedies, including interim awards, as the arbitrator finds necessary to protect the effectiveness of the arbitration proceeding and to promote the fair and expeditious resolution of the controversy, to the same extent and under the same conditions as if the controversy were the subject of a civil action and

(2) a party to an arbitration proceeding may move the court for a provisional remedy only if the matter is urgent and the arbitrator is not able to act timely or the arbitrator cannot provide an adequate remedy.

(c) A party does not waive a right of arbitration by making a [motion] under subsection (a) or (b).

SECTION 9. INITIATION OF ARBITRATION.

(a) A person initiates an arbitration proceeding by giving notice in a record to the other parties to the agreement to arbitrate in the agreed manner between the parties or, in the absence of agreement, by certified or registered mail, return receipt requested and obtained, or by service as authorized for the commencement of a civil action. The notice must describe the nature of the controversy and the remedy sought.

(b) Unless a person objects for lack or insufficiency of notice under Section 15(c) not later than the beginning of the arbitration hearing, the person by appearing at the hearing waives any objection to lack of or insufficiency of notice.

SECTION 10. CONSOLIDATION OF SEPARATE ARBITRATION PROCEEDINGS.

(a) Except as otherwise provided in subsection (c), upon [motion] of a party to an agreement to arbitrate or to an arbitration proceeding, the court may order consolidation of separate arbitration proceedings as to all or some of the claims if:

(1) there are separate agreements to arbitrate or separate arbitration proceedings between the same persons or one of them is a party to a separate agreement to arbitrate or a separate arbitration proceeding with a third person;

(2) the claims subject to the agreements to arbitrate arise in substantial part from the same transaction or series of related transactions;

(3) the existence of a common issue of law or fact creates the possibility of conflicting decisions in the separate arbitration proceedings; and

(4) prejudice resulting from a failure to consolidate is not outweighed by the risk of undue delay or prejudice to the rights of or hardship to parties opposing consolidation.

(b) The court may order consolidation of separate arbitration proceedings as to some claims and allow other claims to be resolved in separate arbitration proceedings.

(c) The court may not order consolidation of the claims of a party to an agreement to arbitrate if the agreement prohibits consolidation.

SECTION 11. APPOINTMENT OF ARBITRATOR; SERVICE AS A NEUTRAL ARBITRATOR.

(a) If the parties to an agreement to arbitrate agree on a method for appointing an arbitrator, that method must be followed, unless the method fails. If the parties have not agreed on a method, the agreed method fails, or an arbitrator appointed fails or is unable to act and a successor has not been appointed, the court, on [motion] of a party to the arbitration proceeding, shall appoint the arbitrator. An arbitrator so appointed has all the powers of an arbitrator designated in the agreement to arbitrate or appointed pursuant to the agreed method.

(b) An individual who has a known, direct, and material interest in the outcome of the arbitration proceeding or a known, existing, and substantial relationship with a party may not serve as an arbitrator required by an agreement to be neutral.

SECTION 12. DISCLOSURE BY ARBITRATOR.

(a) Before accepting appointment, an individual who is requested to serve as an arbitrator, after making a reasonable inquiry, shall disclose to all parties to the agreement to arbitrate and arbitration proceeding and to any other arbitrators any known facts that a reasonable person would consider likely to affect the impartiality of the arbitrator in the arbitration proceeding, including:

(1) a financial or personal interest in the outcome of the arbitration proceeding; and

(2) an existing or past relationship with any of the parties to the agreement to arbitrate or the arbitration proceeding, their counsel or representatives, a witness, or another arbitrators.

(b) An arbitrator has a continuing obligation to disclose to all parties to the agreement to arbitrate and arbitration proceeding and to any other arbitrators any facts that the arbitrator learns after accepting appointment which a reasonable person would consider likely to affect the impartiality of the arbitrator.

(c) If an arbitrator discloses a fact required by subsection (a) or (b) to be disclosed and a party timely objects to the appointment or continued service of the arbitrator based upon the fact disclosed, the objection may be a ground under Section 23(a)(2) for vacating an award made by the arbitrator.

(d) If the arbitrator did not disclose a fact as required by subsection (a) or (b), upon timely objection by a party, the court under Section 23(a)(2) may vacate an award.

(e) An arbitrator appointed as a neutral arbitrator who does not disclose a known, direct, and material interest in the outcome of the arbitration proceeding or a known, existing, and substantial relationship with a party is presumed to act with evident partiality under Section 23(a)(2).

(f) If the parties to an arbitration proceeding agree to the procedures of an arbitration organization or any other procedures for challenges to arbitrators before an award is made, substantial compliance with those procedures is a condition precedent to a [motion] to vacate an award on that ground under Section 23(a)(2).

SECTION 13. ACTION BY MAJORITY.

If there is more than one arbitrator, the powers of an arbitrator must be exercised by a majority of the arbitrators, but all of them shall conduct the hearing under Section 15(c).

SECTION 14. IMMUNITY OF ARBITRATOR; COMPETENCY TO TESTIFY; ATTORNEY'S FEES AND COSTS.

(a) An arbitrator or an arbitration organization acting in that capacity is immune from civil liability to the same extent as a judge of a court of this State acting in a judicial capacity.

(b) The immunity afforded by this section supplements any immunity under other law.

(c) The failure of an arbitrator to make a disclosure required by Section 12 does not cause any loss of immunity under this section.

(d) In a judicial, administrative, or similar proceeding, an arbitrator or representative of an arbitration organization is not competent to testify, and may not be required to produce records as to any statement, conduct, decision, or ruling occurring during the arbitration proceeding, to the same extent as a judge of a court of this State acting in a judicial capacity. This subsection does not apply:

Revised Uniform Arbitration Act (2000)   Appendix H

(1) to the extent necessary to determine the claim of an arbitrator, arbitration organization, or representative of the arbitration organization against a party to the arbitration proceeding; or

(2) to a hearing on a [motion] to vacate an award under Section 23(a)(1) or (2) if the [movant] establishes prima facie that a ground for vacating the award exists.

(e) If a person commences a civil action against an arbitrator, arbitration organization, or representative of an arbitration organization arising from the services of the arbitrator, organization, or representative or if a person seeks to compel an arbitrator or a representative of an arbitration organization to testify or produce records in violation of subsection (d), and the court decides that the arbitrator, arbitration organization, or representative of an arbitration organization is immune from civil liability or that the arbitrator or representative of the organization is not competent to testify, the court shall award to the arbitrator, organization, or representative reasonable attorney's fees and other reasonable expenses of litigation.

SECTION 15. ARBITRATION PROCESS.

(a) An arbitrator may conduct an arbitration in such manner as the arbitrator considers appropriate for a fair and expeditious disposition of the proceeding. The authority conferred upon the arbitrator includes the power to hold conferences with the parties to the arbitration proceeding before the hearing and, among other matters, determine the admissibility, relevance, materiality and weight of any evidence.

(b) An arbitrator may decide a request for summary disposition of a claim or particular issue:

(1) if all interested parties agree; or

(2) upon request of one party to the arbitration proceeding if that party gives notice to all other parties to the proceeding, and the other parties have a reasonable opportunity to respond.

(c) If an arbitrator orders a hearing, the arbitrator shall set a time and place and give notice of the hearing not less than five days before the hearing begins. Unless a party to the arbitration proceeding makes an objection to lack or insufficiency of notice not later than the beginning of the hearing, the party's appearance at the hearing waives the objection. Upon request of a party to the arbitration proceeding and for good cause shown, or upon the arbitrator's own initiative, the arbitrator may adjourn the hearing from time to time as necessary but may not postpone the hearing to a time later than that fixed by the agreement to arbitrate for making the award unless the parties to the arbitration proceeding consent to a later date. The arbitrator may hear and decide the controversy upon the evidence produced although a party who was duly notified of the arbitration proceeding did not appear. The court, on request, may direct the arbitrator to conduct the hearing promptly and render a timely decision.

(d) At a hearing under subsection (c), a party to the arbitration proceeding has a right to be heard, to present evidence material to the controversy, and to cross-examine witnesses appearing at the hearing.

(e) If an arbitrator ceases or is unable to act during the arbitration proceeding, a replacement arbitrator must be appointed in accordance with Section 11 to continue the proceeding and to resolve the controversy.

Section 16. Representation by Lawyer.

A party to an arbitration proceeding may be represented by a lawyer.

Section 17. Witnesses; Subpoenas; Depositions; Discovery.

(a) An arbitrator may issue a subpoena for the attendance of a witness and for the production of records and other evidence at any hearing and may administer oaths. A subpoena must be served in the manner for service of subpoenas in a civil action and, upon [motion] to the court by a party to the arbitration proceeding or the arbitrator, enforced in the manner for enforcement of subpoenas in a civil action.

(b) In order to make the proceedings fair, expeditious, and cost effective, upon request of a party to or a witness in an arbitration proceeding, an arbitrator may permit a deposition of any witness to be taken for use as evidence at the hearing, including a witness who cannot be subpoenaed for or is unable to attend a hearing. The arbitrator shall determine the conditions under which the deposition is taken.

(c) An arbitrator may permit such discovery as the arbitrator decides is appropriate in the circumstances, taking into account the needs of the parties to the arbitration proceeding and other affected persons and the desirability of making the proceeding fair, expeditious, and cost effective.

(d) If an arbitrator permits discovery under subsection (c), the arbitrator may order a party to the arbitration proceeding to comply with the arbitrator's discovery-related orders, issue subpoenas for the attendance of a witness and for the production of records and other evidence at a discovery proceeding, and take action against a noncomplying party to the extent a court could if the controversy were the subject of a civil action in this State.

(e) An arbitrator may issue a protective order to prevent the disclosure of privileged information, confidential information, trade secrets, and other information protected from disclosure to the extent a court could if the controversy were the subject of a civil action in this State.

(f) All laws compelling a person under subpoena to testify and all fees for attending a judicial proceeding, a deposition, or a discovery proceeding as a witness apply to an arbitration proceeding as if the controversy were the subject of a civil action in this State.

(g) The court may enforce a subpoena or discovery-related order for the attendance of a witness within this State and for the production of records and other evidence issued by an arbitrator in connection with an arbitration proceeding in another State upon conditions determined by the court so as to make the arbitration proceeding fair, expeditious, and cost effective. A subpoena or discovery-related order issued by an arbitrator in another State must be served in the manner provided by law for service of subpoenas in a civil action in this State and, upon [motion] to the court by a party to the arbitration proceeding or the arbitrator, enforced in the manner provided by law for enforcement of subpoenas in a civil action in this State.

SECTION 18. JUDICIAL ENFORCEMENT OF PREAWARD RULING BY ARBITRATOR.

If an arbitrator makes a preaward ruling in favor of a party to the arbitration proceeding, the party may request the arbitrator to incorporate the ruling into an award under Section 19. A prevailing party may make a [motion] to the court for an expedited order to confirm the award under Section 22, in which case the court shall summarily decide the [motion]. The court shall issue an order to confirm the award unless the court vacates, modifies, or corrects the award under Section 23 or 24.

SECTION 19. AWARD.

(a) An arbitrator shall make a record of an award. The record must be signed or otherwise authenticated by any arbitrator who concurs with the award. The arbitrator or the arbitration organization shall give notice of the award, including a copy of the award, to each party to the arbitration proceeding.

(b) An award must be made within the time specified by the agreement to arbitrate or, if not specified therein, within the time ordered by the court. The court may extend or the parties to the arbitration proceeding may agree in a record to extend the time. The court or the parties may do so within or after the time specified or ordered. A party waives any objection that an award was not timely made unless the party gives notice of the objection to the arbitrator before receiving notice of the award.

SECTION 20. CHANGE OF AWARD BY ARBITRATOR.

(a) On [motion] to an arbitrator by a party to an arbitration proceeding, the arbitrator may modify or correct an award:

(1) upon a ground stated in Section 24(a)(1) or (3);

(2) because the arbitrator has not made a final and definite award upon a claim submitted by the parties to the arbitration proceeding; or

(3) to clarify the award.

(b) A [motion] under subsection (a) must be made and notice given to all parties within 20 days after the movant receives notice of the award.

(c) A party to the arbitration proceeding must give notice of any objection to the [motion] within 10 days after receipt of the notice.

(d) If a [motion] to the court is pending under Section 22, 23, or 24, the court may submit the claim to the arbitrator to consider whether to modify or correct the award:

(1) upon a ground stated in Section 24(a)(1) or (3);

(2) because the arbitrator has not made a final and definite award upon a claim submitted by the parties to the arbitration proceeding; or

(3) to clarify the award.

(e) An award modified or corrected pursuant to this section is subject to Sections 19(a), 22, 23, and 24.

SECTION 21. REMEDIES; FEES AND EXPENSES OF ARBITRATION PROCEEDING.

(a) An arbitrator may award punitive damages or other exemplary relief if such an award is authorized by law in a civil action involving the same claim and the evidence produced at the hearing justifies the award under the legal standards otherwise applicable to the claim.

(b) An arbitrator may award reasonable attorney's fees and other reasonable expenses of arbitration if such an award is authorized by law in a civil action involving the same claim or by the agreement of the parties to the arbitration proceeding.

(c) As to all remedies other than those authorized by subsections (a) and (b), an arbitrator may order such remedies as the arbitrator considers just and appropriate under the circumstances of the arbitration proceeding. The fact that such a remedy could not or would not be granted by the court is not a ground for refusing to confirm an award under Section 22 or for vacating an award under Section 23.

(d) An arbitrator's expenses and fees, together with other expenses, must be paid as provided in the award.

(e) If an arbitrator awards punitive damages or other exemplary relief under subsection (a), the arbitrator shall specify in the award the basis in fact justifying and the basis in law authorizing the award and state separately the amount of the punitive damages or other exemplary relief.

SECTION 22. CONFIRMATION OF AWARD.

After a party to an arbitration proceeding receives notice of an award, the party may make a [motion] to the court for an order confirming the award at which time the court shall issue a confirming order unless the award is modified or corrected pursuant to Section 20 or 24 or is vacated pursuant to Section 23.

SECTION 23. VACATING AWARD.

(a) Upon [motion] to the court by a party to an arbitration proceeding, the court shall vacate an award made in the arbitration proceeding if:

(1) the award was procured by corruption, fraud, or other undue means;

(2) there was:

(A) evident partiality by an arbitrator appointed as a neutral arbitrator;

(B) corruption by an arbitrator; or

(C) misconduct by an arbitrator prejudicing the rights of a party to the arbitration proceeding;

(3) an arbitrator refused to postpone the hearing upon showing of sufficient cause for postponement, refused to consider evidence material to the controversy, or otherwise conducted the hearing contrary to Section 15, so as to prejudice substantially the rights of a party to the arbitration proceeding;

(4) an arbitrator exceeded the arbitrator's powers;

(5) there was no agreement to arbitrate, unless the person participated in the arbitration proceeding without raising the objection under Section 15(c) not later than the beginning of the arbitration hearing; or

(6) the arbitration was conducted without proper notice of the initiation of an arbitration as required in Section 9 so as to prejudice substantially the rights of a party to the arbitration proceeding.

(b) A [motion] under this section must be filed within 90 days after the [movant] receives notice of the award pursuant to Section 19 or within 90 days after the [movant] receives notice of a modified or corrected award pursuant to Section 20, unless the [movant] alleges that the award was procured by corruption, fraud, or other undue means, in which case the [motion] must be made within 90 days after the ground is known or by the exercise of reasonable care would have been known by the [movant].

(c) If the court vacates an award on a ground other than that set forth in subsection (a)(5), it may order a rehearing. If the award is vacated on a ground stated in subsection (a)(1) or (2), the rehearing must be before a new arbitrator. If the award is vacated on a ground stated in subsection (a)(3), (4), or (6), the rehearing may be before the arbitrator who made the award or the arbitrator's successor. The arbitrator must render the decision in the rehearing within the same time as that provided in Section 19(b) for an award.

(d) If the court denies a [motion] to vacate an award, it shall confirm the award unless a [motion] to modify or correct the award is pending.

SECTION 24. MODIFICATION OR CORRECTION OF AWARD.

(a) Upon [motion] made within 90 days after the [movant] receives notice of the award pursuant to Section 19 or within 90 days after the [movant] receives notice of a modified or corrected award pursuant to Section 20, the court shall modify or correct the award if:

(1) there was an evident mathematical miscalculation or an evident mistake in the description of a person, thing, or property referred to in the award;

(2) the arbitrator has made an award on a claim not submitted to the arbitrator and the award may be corrected without affecting the merits of the decision upon the claims submitted; or

(3) the award is imperfect in a matter of form not affecting the merits of the decision on the claims submitted.

(b) If a [motion] made under subsection (a) is granted, the court shall modify or correct and confirm the award as modified or corrected. Otherwise, unless a motion to vacate is pending, the court shall confirm the award.

(c) A [motion] to modify or correct an award pursuant to this section may be joined with a [motion] to vacate the award.

SECTION 25. JUDGMENT ON AWARD; ATTORNEY'S FEES AND LITIGATION EXPENSES.

(a) Upon granting an order confirming, vacating without directing a rehearing, modifying, or correcting an award, the court shall enter a judgment in conformity therewith. The judgment may be recorded, docketed, and enforced as any other judgment in a civil action.

(b) A court may allow reasonable costs of the [motion] and subsequent judicial proceedings.

(c) On [application] of a prevailing party to a contested judicial proceeding under Section 22, 23, or 24, the court may add reasonable attorney's fees and other reasonable expenses of litigation incurred in a judicial proceeding after the award is made to a judgment confirming, vacating without directing a rehearing, modifying, or correcting an award.

Section 26. Jurisdiction.

(a) A court of this State having jurisdiction over the controversy and the parties may enforce an agreement to arbitrate.

(b) An agreement to arbitrate providing for arbitration in this State confers exclusive jurisdiction on the court to enter judgment on an award under this [Act].

Section 27. Venue.

A [motion] pursuant to Section 5 must be made in the court of the [county] in which the agreement to arbitrate specifies the arbitration hearing is to be held or, if the hearing has been held, in the court of the [county] in which it was held. Otherwise, the [motion] may be made in the court of any [county] in which an adverse party resides or has a place of business or, if no adverse party has a residence or place of business in this State, in the court of any [county] in this State. All subsequent [motions] must be made in the court hearing the initial [motion] unless the court otherwise directs.

Section 28. Appeals.

(a) An appeal may be taken from:
    (1) an order denying a [motion] to compel arbitration;
    (2) an order granting a [motion] to stay arbitration;
    (3) an order confirming or denying confirmation of an award;
    (4) an order modifying or correcting an award;
    (5) an order vacating an award without directing a rehearing; or
    (6) a final judgment entered pursuant to this [Act].

(b) An appeal under this section must be taken as from an order or a judgment in a civil action.

Section 29. Uniformity of Application and Construction.

In applying and construing this uniform act, consideration must be given to the need to promote uniformity of the law with respect to its subject matter among States that enact it.

Appendix H — Revised Uniform Arbitration Act (2000)

SECTION 30. ELECTRONIC SIGNATURES IN GLOBAL AND NATIONAL COMMERCE ACT.

The provisions of this [Act] governing the legal effect, validity, or enforceability of electronic records or signatures, and of contracts formed or performed with the use of such records or signatures conform to the requirements of Section 102 of the Electronic Signatures in Global and National Commerce Act, Pub. L. No. 106-229, 114 Stat. 464 (2000), and supersede, modify, and limit the Electronic Signatures in Global and National Commerce Act.

SECTION 31. EFFECTIVE DATE.

This [Act] takes effect on [effective date].

SECTION 32. REPEAL.

Effective on [delayed date should be the same as that in Section 3(c)], the [Uniform Arbitration Act] is repealed.

SECTION 33. SAVINGS CLAUSE.

This [Act] does not affect an action or proceeding commenced or right accrued before this [Act] takes effect. Subject to Section 3 of this [Act], an arbitration agreement made before the effective date of this [Act] is governed by the [Uniform Arbitration Act].

Appendix I
MODEL STANDARDS OF PRACTICE FOR FAMILY AND DIVORCE MEDIATION (2001)[1]

OVERVIEW AND DEFINITIONS

Family and divorce mediation ("family mediation" or "mediation") is a process in which a mediator, an impartial third party, facilitates the resolution of family disputes by promoting the participants' voluntary agreement. The family mediator assists communication, encourages understanding and focuses the participants on their individual and common interests. The family mediator works with the participants to explore options, make decisions and reach their own agreements.

Family mediation is not a substitute for the need for family members to obtain independent legal advice or counseling or therapy. Nor is it appropriate for all families. However, experience has established that family mediation is a valuable option for many families because it can:

- increase the self-determination of participants and their ability to communicate;
- promote the best interests of children; and
- reduce the economic and emotional costs associated with the resolution of family disputes.

Effective mediation requires that the family mediator be qualified by training, experience and temperament; that the mediator be impartial; that the participants

---

1. A copy of the Model Standards of Practice for Family and Divorce Mediation, adopted by the ABA House of Delegates in February 2001, may be found in 35 Fam. L. Q. 27 (2001).

Model Standards of Practice for Family and Divorce Mediation   Appendix I

reach their decisions voluntarily; that their decisions be based on sufficient factual data; that the mediator be aware of the impact of culture and diversity; and that the best interests of children be taken into account. Further, the mediator should also be prepared to identify families whose history includes domestic abuse or child abuse.

These Model Standards of Practice for Family and Divorce Mediation ("Model Standards") aim to perform three major functions:

1. to serve as a guide for the conduct of family mediators;
2. to inform the mediating participants of what they can expect; and
3. to promote public confidence in mediation as a process for resolving family disputes.

The Model Standards are aspirational in character. They describe good practices for family mediators. They are not intended to create legal rules or standards of liability.

The Model Standards include different levels of guidance:

- Use of the term "may" in a Standard is the lowest strength of guidance and indicates a practice that the family mediator should consider adopting but which can be deviated from in the exercise of good professional judgment.
- Most of the Standards employ the term "should" which indicates that the practice described in the Standard is highly desirable and should be departed from only with very strong reason.
- The rarer use of the term "shall" in a Standard is a higher level of guidance to the family mediator, indicating that the mediator should not have discretion to depart from the practice described.

STANDARD I

A family mediator shall recognize that mediation is based on the principle of self-determination by the participants.

A. Self-determination is the fundamental principle of family mediation. The mediation process relies upon the ability of participants to make their own voluntary and informed decisions.

B. The primary role of a family mediator is to assist the participants to gain a better understanding of their own needs and interests and the needs and interests of others and to facilitate agreement among the participants.

C. A family mediator should inform the participants that they may seek information and advice from a variety of sources during the mediation process.

Appendix I Model Standards of Practice for Family and Divorce Mediation

D. A family mediator shall inform the participants that they may withdraw from family mediation at any time and are not required to reach an agreement in mediation.

E. The family mediator's commitment shall be to the participants and the process. Pressure from outside of the mediation process shall never influence the mediator to coerce participants to settle.

STANDARD II

A family mediator shall be qualified by education and training to undertake the mediation.

A. To perform the family mediator's role, a mediator should:

1. have knowledge of family law;

2. have knowledge of and training in the impact of family conflict on parents, children and other participants, including knowledge of child development, domestic abuse and child abuse and neglect;

3. have education and training specific to the process of mediation;

4. be able to recognize the impact of culture and diversity.

B. Family mediators should provide information to the participants about the mediator's relevant training, education and expertise.

STANDARD III

A family mediator shall facilitate the participants' understanding of what mediation is and assess their capacity to mediate before the participants reach an agreement to mediate.

A. Before family mediation begins a mediator should provide the participants with an overview of the process and its purposes, including:

1. informing the participants that reaching an agreement in family mediation is consensual in nature, that a mediator is an impartial facilitator, and that a mediator may not impose or force any settlement on the parties;

2. distinguishing family mediation from other processes designed to address family issues and disputes;

3. informing the participants that any agreements reached will be reviewed by the court when court approval is required;

4. informing the participants that they may obtain independent advice from attorneys, counsel, advocates, accountants, therapists or other professionals during the mediation process;

5. advising the participants, in appropriate cases, that they can seek the advice of religious figures, elders or other significant persons in their community whose opinions they value;

6. discussing, if applicable, the issue of separate sessions with the participants, a description of the circumstances in which the mediator may meet alone with any of the participants, or with any third party and the conditions of confidentiality concerning these separate sessions;

7. informing the participants that the presence or absence of other persons at a mediation, including attorneys, counselors or advocates, depends on the agreement of the participants and the mediator, unless a statute or regulation otherwise requires or the mediator believes that the presence of another person is required or may be beneficial because of a history or threat of violence or other serious coercive activity by a participant;

8. describing the obligations of the mediator to maintain the confidentiality of the mediation process and its results as well as any exceptions to confidentiality;

9. advising the participants of the circumstances under which the mediator may suspend or terminate the mediation process and that a participant has a right to suspend or terminate mediation at any time.

B. The participants should sign a written agreement to mediate their dispute and the terms and conditions thereof within a reasonable time after first consulting the family mediator.

C. The family mediator should be alert to the capacity and willingness of the participants to mediate before proceeding with the mediation and throughout the process. A mediator should not agree to conduct the mediation if the mediator reasonably believes one or more of the participants is unable or unwilling to participate;

D. Family mediators should not accept a dispute for mediation if they cannot satisfy the expectations of the participants concerning the timing of the process.

STANDARD IV

A family mediator shall conduct the mediation process in an impartial manner. A family mediator shall disclose all actual and potential grounds of bias and conflicts of interest reasonably known to the mediator. The participants shall be free to retain the mediator by an informed, written waiver of the conflict of interest. However, if a bias or conflict of interest clearly impairs a mediator's impartiality, the mediator shall withdraw regardless of the express agreement of the participants.

A. Impartiality means freedom from favoritism or bias in word, action or appearance, and includes a commitment to assist all participants as opposed to any one individual.

Appendix I Model Standards of Practice for Family and Divorce Mediation

B. Conflict of interest means any relationship between the mediator, any participant or the subject matter of the dispute, that compromises or appears to compromise the mediator's impartiality.

C. A family mediator should not accept a dispute for mediation if the family mediator cannot be impartial.

D. A family mediator should identify and disclose potential grounds of bias or conflict of interest upon which a mediator's impartiality might reasonably be questioned. Such disclosure should be made prior to the start of a mediation and in time to allow the participants to select an alternate mediator.

E. A family mediator should resolve all doubts in favor of disclosure. All disclosures should be made as soon as practical after the mediator becomes aware of the bias or potential conflict of interest. The duty to disclose is a continuing duty.

F. A family mediator should guard against bias or partiality based on the participants' personal characteristics, background or performance at the mediation.

G. A family mediator should avoid conflicts of interest in recommending the services of other professionals.

H. A family mediator shall not use information about participants obtained in a mediation for personal gain or advantage.

I. A family mediator should withdraw pursuant to Standard IX if the mediator believes the mediator's impartiality has been compromised or a conflict of interest has been identified and has not been waived by the participants.

STANDARD V

A family mediator shall fully disclose and explain the basis of any compensation, fees and charges to the participants.

A. The participants should be provided with sufficient information about fees at the outset of mediation to determine if they wish to retain the services of the mediator.

B. The participants' written agreement to mediate their dispute should include a description of their fee arrangement with the mediator.

C. A mediator should not enter into a fee agreement that is contingent upon the results of the mediation or the amount of the settlement.

D. A mediator should not accept a fee for referral of a matter to another mediator or to any other person.

E. Upon termination of mediation a mediator should return any unearned fee to the participants.

STANDARD VI

A family mediator shall structure the mediation process so that the participants make decisions based on sufficient information and knowledge.

A. The mediator should facilitate full and accurate disclosure and the acquisition and development of information during mediation so that the participants can make informed decisions. This may be accomplished by encouraging participants to consult appropriate experts.

B. Consistent with standards of impartiality and preserving participant self-determination, a mediator may provide the participants with information that the mediator is qualified by training or experience to provide. The mediator shall not provide therapy or legal advice.

C. The mediator should recommend that the participants obtain independent legal representation before concluding an agreement.

D. If the participants so desire, the mediator should allow attorneys, counsel or advocates for the participants to be present at the mediation sessions.

E. With the agreement of the participants, the mediator may document the participants' resolution of their dispute. The mediator should inform the participants that any agreement should be reviewed by an independent attorney before it is signed.

STANDARD VII

A family mediator shall maintain the confidentiality of all information acquired in the mediation process, unless the mediator is permitted or required to reveal the information by law or agreement of the participants.

A. The mediator should discuss the participants' expectations of confidentiality with them prior to undertaking the mediation. The written agreement to mediate should include provisions concerning confidentiality.

B. Prior to undertaking the mediation the mediator should inform the participants of the limitations of confidentiality such as statutory, judicially or ethically mandated reporting.

C. As permitted by law, the mediator shall disclose a participant's threat of suicide or violence against any person to the threatened person and the appropriate authorities if the mediator believes such threat is likely to be acted upon.

D. If the mediator holds private sessions with a participant, the obligations of confidentiality concerning those sessions should be discussed and agreed upon prior to the sessions.

Appendix I   Model Standards of Practice for Family and Divorce Mediation

E. If subpoenaed or otherwise noticed to testify or to produce documents the mediator should inform the participants immediately. The mediator should not testify or provide documents in response to a subpoena without an order of the court if the mediator reasonably believes doing so would violate an obligation of confidentiality to the participants.

STANDARD VIII

A family mediator shall assist participants in determining how to promote the best interests of children.

A. The mediator should encourage the participants to explore the range of options available for separation or post-divorce parenting arrangements and their respective costs and benefits. Referral to a specialist in child development may be appropriate for these purposes. The topics for discussion may include, among others:

1. information about community resources and programs that can help the participants and their children cope with the consequences of family reorganization and family violence;

2. problems that continuing conflict creates for children's development and what steps might be taken to ameliorate the effects of conflict on the children;

3. development of a parenting plan that covers the children's physical residence and decision-making responsibilities for the children, with appropriate levels of detail as agreed to by the participants;

4. the possible need to revise parenting plans as the developmental needs of the children evolve over time; and

5. encouragement to the participants to develop appropriate dispute resolution mechanisms to facilitate future revisions of the parenting plan.

B. The mediator should be sensitive to the impact of culture and religion on parenting philosophy and other decisions.

C. The mediator shall inform any court-appointed representative for the children of the mediation. If a representative for the children participates, the mediator should, at the outset, discuss the effect of that participation on the mediation process and the confidentiality of the mediation with the participants. Whether the representative of the children participates or not, the mediator shall provide the representative with the resulting agreements insofar as they relate to the children.

D. Except in extraordinary circumstances, the children should not participate in the mediation process without the consent of both parents and the children's court-appointed representative.

Model Standards of Practice for Family and Divorce Mediation   Appendix I

E. Prior to including the children in the mediation process, the mediator should consult with the parents and the children's court-appointed representative about whether the children should participate in the mediation process and the form of that participation.

F. The mediator should inform all concerned about the available options for the children's participation (which may include personal participation, an interview with a mental health professional, the mediator interviewing the child and reporting to the parents, or a videotaped statement by the child) and discuss the costs and benefits of each with the participants.

STANDARD IX

A family mediator shall recognize a family situation involving child abuse or neglect and take appropriate steps to shape the mediation process accordingly.

A. As used in these Standards, child abuse or neglect is defined by applicable state law.

B. A mediator shall not undertake a mediation in which the family situation has been assessed to involve child abuse or neglect without appropriate and adequate training.

C. If the mediator has reasonable grounds to believe that a child of the participants is abused or neglected within the meaning of the jurisdiction's child abuse and neglect laws, the mediator shall comply with applicable child protection laws.

   1. The mediator should encourage the participants to explore appropriate services for the family.

   2. The mediator should consider the appropriateness of suspending or terminating the mediation process in light of the allegations.

STANDARD X

A family mediator shall recognize a family situation involving domestic abuse and take appropriate steps to shape the mediation process accordingly.

A. As used in these Standards, domestic abuse includes domestic violence as defined by applicable state law and issues of control and intimidation.

B. A mediator shall not undertake a mediation in which the family situation has been assessed to involve domestic abuse without appropriate and adequate training.

Appendix I   Model Standards of Practice for Family and Divorce Mediation

C. Some cases are not suitable for mediation because of safety, control or intimidation issues. A mediator should make a reasonable effort to screen for the existence of domestic abuse prior to entering into an agreement to mediate. The mediator should continue to assess for domestic abuse throughout the mediation process.

D. If domestic abuse appears to be present the mediator shall consider taking measures to insure the safety of participants and the mediator including, among others:

   1. establishing appropriate security arrangements;

   2. holding separate sessions with the participants even without the agreement of all participants;

   3. allowing a friend, representative, advocate, counsel or attorney to attend the mediation sessions;

   4. encouraging the participants to be represented by an attorney, counsel or an advocate throughout the mediation process;

   5. referring the participants to appropriate community resources;

   6. suspending or terminating the mediation sessions, with appropriate steps to protect the safety of the participants.

E. The mediator should facilitate the participants' formulation of parenting plans that protect the physical safety and psychological well-being of themselves and their children.

STANDARD XI

A family mediator shall suspend or terminate the mediation process when the mediator reasonably believes that a participant is unable to effectively participate or for other compelling reason.

A. Circumstances under which a mediator should consider suspending or terminating the mediation, may include, among others:

   1. the safety of a participant or well-being of a child is threatened;

   2. a participant has or is threatening to abduct a child;

   3. a participant is unable to participate due to the influence of drugs, alcohol, or physical or mental condition;

   4. the participants are about to enter into an agreement that the mediator reasonably believes to be unconscionable;

   5. a participant is using the mediation to further illegal conduct;

   6. a participant is using the mediation process to gain an unfair advantage;

   7. if the mediator believes the mediator's impartiality has been compromised in accordance with Standard IV.

B. If the mediator does suspend or terminate the mediation, the mediator should take all reasonable steps to minimize prejudice or inconvenience to the participants which may result.

STANDARD XII

A family mediator shall be truthful in the advertisement and solicitation for mediation.

A. Mediators should refrain from promises and guarantees of results. A mediator should not advertise statistical settlement data or settlement rates.

B. Mediators should accurately represent their qualifications. In an advertisement or other communication, a mediator may make reference to meeting state, national or private organizational qualifications only if the entity referred to has a procedure for qualifying mediators and the mediator has been duly granted the requisite status.

STANDARD XIII

A family mediator shall acquire and maintain professional competence in mediation.

A. Mediators should continuously improve their professional skills and abilities by, among other activities, participating in relevant continuing education programs and should regularly engage in self-assessment.

B. Mediators should participate in programs of peer consultation and should help train and mentor the work of less experienced mediators.

C. Mediators should continuously strive to understand the impact of culture and diversity on the mediator's practice.

Appendix J
UNIFORM MEDIATION ACT (2002)**

PREFATORY NOTE

... [L]aws play a limited but important role in encouraging the effective use of mediation and maintaining its integrity, as well as the appropriate relationship of mediation with the justice system. In particular, the law has the unique capacity to assure that the reasonable expectations of participants regarding the confidentiality of the mediation process are met, rather than frustrated. For this reason, a central thrust of the Act is to provide a privilege that assures confidentiality in legal proceedings (*see* Sections 4-6). Because the privilege makes it more difficult to offer evidence to challenge the settlement agreement, the Drafters viewed the issue of confidentiality as tied to provisions that will help increase the likelihood that the mediation process will be fair. Fairness is enhanced if it will be conducted with integrity and the parties' knowing consent will be preserved. The Act protects integrity and knowing consent through provisions that provide exceptions to the privilege (Section 6), limit disclosures by the mediator to judges and others who may rule on the case (Section 7), require mediators to disclose conflicts of interest (Section 9), and assure that parties may bring a lawyer or other support person to the mediation session (Section 10). In some limited ways, the law can also encourage the use of mediation as part of the policy to promote the private resolution of disputes through informed self-determination. A uniform act that promotes predictability and simplicity may encourage greater use of mediation. . . .

**Editors' Note: The National Conference of Commissioners on Uniform State Law consists of lawyers appointed by the official designated by statute in each state, often the governor, to represent that state in the development, drafting, and adoption of uniform and model legislation. The Conference has approved many other uniform acts, including the Uniform Commercial Code and the Revised Uniform Arbitration Act. The Uniform Mediation Act was drafted in cooperation with a similar committee representing the American Bar Association Section on Dispute Resolution. Most citations in the comments have been omitted here. The full text including comments is posted at *www.law.upenn.edu/bll/ulc/ulc_frame.htm*.

At the same time, it is important to avoid laws that diminish the creative and diverse use of mediation. The Act promotes the autonomy of the parties by leaving to them those matters that can be set by agreement and need not be set inflexibly by statute. In addition, some provisions in the Act may be varied by party agreement, as specified in the comments to the sections. . . .

1. PROMOTING CANDOR

Candor during mediation is encouraged by maintaining the parties' and mediators' expectations regarding confidentiality of mediation communications. *See* Sections 4-6. Virtually all state legislatures have recognized the necessity of protecting mediation confidentiality to encourage the effective use of mediation to resolve disputes. Indeed, state legislatures have enacted more than 250 mediation privilege statutes. Approximately half of the States have enacted privilege statutes that apply generally to mediations in the State, while the other half include privileges within the provisions of statutes establishing mediation programs for specific substantive legal issues, such as employment or human rights.

The Drafters recognize that mediators typically promote a candid and informal exchange regarding events in the past, as well as the parties' perceptions of and attitudes toward these events, and that mediators encourage parties to think constructively and creatively about ways in which their differences might be resolved. This frank exchange can be achieved only if the participants know that what is said in the mediation will not be used to their detriment through later court proceedings and other adjudicatory processes. . . . This rationale has sometimes been extended to mediators to encourage mediators to be candid with the parties by allowing the mediator to block evidence of the mediator's notes and other statements by the mediator. *See, e.g.*, Ohio Rev. Code Ann. §2317.023 (West 1996).

Similarly, public confidence in and the voluntary use of mediation can be expected to expand if people have confidence that the mediator will not take sides or disclose their statements, particularly in the context of other investigations or judicial processes. The public confidence rationale has been extended to permit the mediator to object to testifying, so that the mediator will not be viewed as biased in future mediation sessions that involve comparable parties. *See, e.g., NLRB v. Macaluso*, 618 F.2d 51 (9th Cir. 1980) (public interest in maintaining the perceived and actual impartiality of mediators outweighs the benefits derivable from a given mediator's testimony). To maintain public confidence in the fairness of mediation, a number of States prohibit a mediator from disclosing mediation communications to a judge or other officials in a position to affect the decision in a case. This justification also is reflected in standards [that prohibit] the use of a threat of disclosure or recommendation to pressure the parties to accept a particular settlement.

A statute is required only to assure that aspect of confidentiality that relates to evidence compelled in a judicial and other legal proceeding. The parties can rely on the mediator's assurance of confidentiality in terms of mediator disclosures outside the proceedings, as the mediator would be liable for a breach of such an assurance. Also, the parties can expect enforcement of their agreement to keep things confidential through contract damages and sometimes specific enforcement. The courts have also enforced court orders or rules regarding nondisclosure through orders striking pleadings and fining lawyers. Promises, contracts, and court rules or orders are unavailing, however, with respect to discovery, trial, and otherwise compelled or subpoenaed evidence. Assurance with respect to this aspect of confidentiality has rarely been accorded by common law. Thus, the major contribution of the Act is to provide a privilege in legal proceedings, where it would otherwise either not be available or would not be available in a uniform way across the States.

As with other privileges, the mediation privilege must have limits, and nearly all existing state mediation statutes provide them. Definitions and exceptions primarily are necessary to give appropriate weight to other valid justice system values, in addition to those already discussed in this Section. They often apply to situations that arise only rarely, but might produce grave injustice in that unusual case if not excepted from the privilege.

Finally . . . [a] uniform and generic privilege makes it easier for the parties and mediators to understand what law will apply and therefore to understand the coverage and limits of the Act, so that they can conduct themselves in a mediation accordingly.

2. ENCOURAGING RESOLUTION IN ACCORDANCE WITH OTHER PRINCIPLES

. . . The primary guarantees of fairness within mediation are the integrity of the process and informed self-determination. Self-determination also contributes to party satisfaction. Consensual dispute resolution allows parties to tailor not only the result but also the process to their needs, with minimal intervention by the State. . . .

Self-determination is encouraged by provisions that limit the potential for coercion of the parties to accept settlements, *see* Section 9(a), and that allow parties to have counsel or other support persons present during the mediation session. *See* Section 10. The Act promotes the integrity of the mediation process by requiring the mediator to disclose conflicts of interest, and to be candid about qualifications. *See* Section 9.

3. IMPORTANCE OF UNIFORMITY

This Act is designed to simplify a complex area of the law. Currently, legal rules affecting mediation can be found in more than 2500 statutes. Many of these statutes can be replaced by the Act, which applies a generic approach to topics that are covered in varying ways by a number of specific statutes currently scattered within substantive provisions. . . .

6. DRAFTING PHILOSOPHY

Mediation often involves both parties and mediators from a variety of professions and backgrounds, many of who are not attorneys or represented by counsel. With this in mind, the Drafters sought to make the provisions accessible and understandable to readers from a variety of backgrounds, sometimes keeping the Act shorter by leaving some discretion in the courts to apply the provisions in accordance with the general purposes of the Act, delineated and expanded upon in Section 1 of this Prefatory Note. These policies include fostering prompt, economical, and amicable resolution, integrity in the process, self-determination by parties, candor in negotiations, societal needs for information, and uniformity of law.

The Drafters sought to avoid including in the Act those types of provisions that should vary by type of program or legal context and that were therefore more appropriately left to program-specific statutes or rules. Mediator qualifications, for example, are not prescribed by this Act. The Drafters also recognized that some general standards are often better applied through those who administer ethical standards or local rules, where an advisory opinion might be sought to guide persons faced with immediate uncertainty. Where individual choice or notice was important to allow for self-determination or avoid a trap for the unwary, such as for nondisclosure by the parties outside the context of proceedings, the Drafters left the matter largely to local rule or contract among the participants. As the result, the Act largely governs those narrow circumstances in which the mediation process comes into contact with formal legal processes.

SECTION 1. TITLE.

This [Act] may be cited as the Uniform Mediation Act.

SECTION 2. DEFINITIONS.

In this [Act]:

(1) "Mediation" means a process in which a mediator facilitates communication and negotiation between parties to assist them in reaching a voluntary agreement regarding their dispute.

(2) "Mediation communication" means a statement, whether oral or in a record or verbal or nonverbal, that occurs during a mediation or is made for purposes of considering, conducting, participating in, initiating, continuing, or reconvening a mediation or retaining a mediator.

(3) "Mediator" means an individual who conducts a mediation.

(4) "Nonparty participant" means a person, other than a party or mediator, that participates in a mediation.

(5) "Mediation party" means a person that participates in a mediation and whose agreement is necessary to resolve the dispute.

(6) "Person" means an individual, corporation, business trust, estate, trust, partnership, limited liability company, association, joint venture, government; governmental subdivision, agency, or instrumentality; public corporation, or any other legal or commercial entity.

(7) "Proceeding" means:

(A) a judicial, administrative, arbitral, or other adjudicative process, including related pre-hearing and post-hearing motions, conferences, and discovery; or

(B) a legislative hearing or similar process.

(8) "Record" means information that is inscribed on a tangible medium or that is stored in an electronic or other medium and is retrievable in perceivable form.

(9) "Sign" means:

(A) to execute or adopt a tangible symbol with the present intent to authenticate a record; or

(B) to attach or logically associate an electronic symbol, sound, or process to or with a record with the present intent to authenticate a record.

Reporter's Notes

2. Section 2(2). "MediationCommunication."

Mediation communications are statements that are made orally, through conduct, or in writing or other recorded activity. This definition is aimed primarily at the privilege provisions of Sections 4-6. It is similar to the general rule, as reflected in Uniform Rule of Evidence 801, which defines a "statement" as "an oral or written assertion or nonverbal conduct of an individual who intends it as an assertion." Most generic mediation privileges cover communications but do not cover conduct that is not intended as an assertion. The mere fact that a person attended the mediation—in other words, the physical presence of a person—is not a communication. By contrast, nonverbal conduct such as nodding in response to a question would be a "communication" because it is meant as an assertion; however nonverbal conduct such as smoking a cigarette during the mediation session typically would not be a "communication" because it was not meant by the actor as an assertion.

A mediator's mental impressions and observations about the mediation present a more complicated question, with important practical implications. *See Olam v. Congress Mortgage Co.*, 68 F.Supp. 2d 1110 (N.D. Cal. 1999). As discussed below, the mediation privilege is modeled after, and draws heavily upon, the attorney-client privilege, a strong privilege that is supported by well-developed case law. Courts are to be expected to look to that well developed body of law in construing this Act. In this regard, mental impressions that are based even in part on mediation communications would generally be protected by privilege.

More specifically, communications include both statements and conduct meant to inform, because the purpose of the privilege is to promote candid mediation communications. By analogy to the attorney-client privilege, silence in response to a question may be a communication, if it is meant to inform. Further, conduct meant to explain or communicate a fact, such as the re-enactment of an accident, is a communication. Similarly, a client's revelation of a hidden scar to an attorney in response to a question is a communication if meant to inform. In contrast, a purely physical phenomenon, such as a tattoo or the color of a suit of clothes, observable by all, is not a communication.

If evidence of mental impressions would reveal, even indirectly, mediation communications, then that evidence would be blocked by the privilege. For example, a mediator's mental impressions of the capacity of a mediation participant to enter into a binding mediated settlement agreement would be privileged if that impression was in part based on the statements that the party made during the mediation, because the testimony might reveal the content or character of the mediation communications upon which the impression is based. In contrast, the mental impression would not be privileged if it was based exclusively on the mediator's observation of that party wearing heavy clothes and an overcoat on a hot summer day because the choice of clothing was not meant to inform.

There is no justification for making readily observable conduct privileged, certainly not more privileged than it is under the attorney-client privilege. If the conduct is seen in the mediation room, it can also be observed, even photographed, outside of the mediation room, as well as in other contexts. One of the primary reasons for making mediation communications privileged is to promote candor, and excluding evidence of a readily observable characteristic is not necessary to promote candor. . . .

SECTION 3. SCOPE.

(a) Except as otherwise provided in subsection (b) or (c), this [Act] applies to a mediation in which:

(1) the mediation parties are required to mediate by statute or court or administrative agency rule or referred to mediation by a court, administrative agency, or arbitrator;

(2) the mediation parties and the mediator agree to mediate in a record that demonstrates an expectation that mediation communications will be privileged against disclosure; or

(3) the mediation parties use as a mediator an individual who holds himself or herself out as a mediator or the mediation is provided by a person that holds itself out as providing mediation.

(b) The [Act] does not apply to a mediation:

(1) relating to the establishment, negotiation, administration, or termination of a collective bargaining relationship;

(2) relating to a dispute that is pending under or is part of the processes established by a collective bargaining agreement, except that the [Act] applies to a mediation arising out of a dispute that has been filed with an administrative agency or court;

(3) conducted by a judge who might make a ruling on the case; or

(4) conducted under the auspices of:

(A) a primary or secondary school if all the parties are students or

(B) a correctional institution for youths if all the parties are residents of that institution.

(c) If the parties agree in advance in a signed record, or a record of proceeding reflects agreement by the parties, that all or part of a mediation is not privileged, the privileges under Sections 4 through 6 do not apply to the mediation or part agreed upon. However, Sections 4 through 6 apply to a mediation communication made by a person that has not received actual notice of the agreement before the communication is made.

Reporter's Notes

1. *In general.*

The Act is broad in its coverage of mediation, a departure from the common state statutes that apply to mediation in particular contexts, such as court-connected mediation or community mediation, or to the mediation of particular types of disputes, such as worker's compensation or civil rights. Moreover, unlike many mediation privileges, it also applies in some contexts in which the Rules of Evidence are not consistently followed, such as administrative hearings and arbitration.

Whether the Act in fact applies is a crucial issue because it determines not only the application of the mediation privilege but also whether the mediator has the obligations regarding the disclosure of conflicts of interest and, if asked, qualifications in Section 9; is prohibited from making disclosures about the mediation to courts, agencies and investigative authorities in Section 7; and must accommodate requirements regarding accompanying individuals in Section 10. . . .

2. *Section 3(a). Mediations covered by Act; triggering mechanisms.*

Section 3(a) sets forth three conditions, the satisfaction of any one of which will trigger the application of the Act. This triggering requirement is necessary because the many different forms, contexts, and practices of mediation and other methods of dispute resolution make it sometimes difficult to know with certainty whether one is engaged in a mediation or some other dispute resolution or prevention process that employs mediation and related principles. This problem is exacerbated by the fact that unlike other professionals—such as doctors, lawyers, and social workers—mediators are not licensed and the process they conduct is informal. If the intent to mediate is not clear, even a casual discussion over a backyard fence might later be deemed to have been a mediation, unfairly surprising those involved and frustrating the reasonable expectations of the parties.

[T]he Drafting Committees discussed whether it should cover the many cultural and religious practices that are similar to mediation and that use a person similar to the mediator, as defined in this Act. On the one hand, many of these cultural and religious practices, like more traditional mediation, streamline and resolve conflicts, while solving problems and restoring relationships. Some examples of these practices are Ho'oponopono, circle ceremonies, family conferencing, and pastoral or marital counseling. These cultural and religious practices bring richness to the quality of life and contribute to traditional mediation. On the other hand, there are instances in which the application of the Act to these practices would be disruptive of the practices and therefore undesirable. On balance, furthering the principle of self-determination, the Drafting Committees decided that those involved should make the choice to be covered by the Act in those instances in which other definitional requirements of Section 2 are met by entering into an agreement to mediate reflected by a record or securing a court or agency referral pursuant to Section 3(a)(1). At the same time, these persons could opt out the Act's coverage by not using this triggering mechanism. This leaves a great deal of leeway, appropriately, with those involved in the practices. . . .

Appendix J   **Uniform Mediation Act (2002)**

7. Section 3(c). Alternative of non-privileged mediation.

This Section allows the parties to opt for a non-privileged mediation or mediation session by mutual agreement, and furthers the Act's policy of party self-determination. If the parties so agree, the privilege sections of the Act do not apply, thus fulfilling the parties' reasonable expectations regarding the confidentiality of that mediation or session. For example, parties in a sophisticated commercial mediation, who are represented by counsel, may see no need for a privilege to attach to a mediation or session, and may by express written agreement "opt out" of the Act's privilege provisions. Similarly, parties may also use this option if they wish to rely on, and therefore use in evidence, statements made during the mediation. It is the parties rather than the mediator who make this choice, although a mediator could presumably refuse to mediate a mediation or session that is not covered by this Act. Even if the parties do not agree in advance, the parties, mediator, and all nonparty participants can waive the privilege pursuant to Section 5. In this instance, however, the mediator and other participants can block the waiver in some respects.

If the parties want to opt out, they should inform the mediators or nonparty participants of this agreement, because without actual notice, the privileges of the Act still apply to the mediation communications of the persons who have not been so informed until such notice is actually received. . . .

Section 4. Privilege Against Disclosure; Admissibility; Discovery.

(a) Except as otherwise provided in Section 6, a mediation communication is privileged as provided in subsection (b) and is not subject to discovery or admissible in evidence in a proceeding unless waived or precluded as provided by Section 5.

(b) In a proceeding, the following privileges apply:

    (1) A mediation party may refuse to disclose, and may prevent any other person from disclosing, a mediation communication.

    (2) A mediator may refuse to disclose a mediation communication, and may prevent any other person from disclosing a mediation communication of the mediator.

    (3) A nonparty participant may refuse to disclose, and may prevent any other person from disclosing, a mediation communication of the nonparty participant.

(c) Evidence or information that is otherwise admissible or subject to discovery does not become inadmissible or protected from discovery solely by reason of its disclosure or use in a mediation.

Reporter's Notes

4. Section 4(b). Operation of privilege. . . .

a. The holders of the privilege.

1. In general.

A critical component of the Act's general rule is its designation of the holder—i.e., the person who is eligible to raise and waive the privilege. . . . Those statutes that designate a holder tend to be split between those that make the parties the only holders of the privilege, and those that also make the mediator a holder. The Act adopts an approach that provides that both the parties and the mediators may assert the privilege regarding certain matters, thus giving weight to the primary concern of each rationale.

2. Parties as holders.

The mediation privilege of the parties draws upon the purpose, rationale, and traditions of the attorney-client privilege, in that its paramount justification is to encourage candor by the mediation parties, just as encouraging the client's candor is the central justification for the attorney-client privilege. . . . It should be noted that even if the mediator loses the privilege to block or assert a privilege, the parties may still come forward and assert their privilege, thus blocking the mediator who has lost the privilege from providing testimony about the affected mediation. . . .

3. Mediators as holders.

Mediators are made holders with respect to their own mediation communications, so that they may participate candidly, and with respect to their own testimony, so that they will not be viewed as biased in future mediations. . . .

4. Nonparty participants as holders.

In addition, the Act adds a privilege for the nonparty participant, though limited to the communications by that individual in the mediation. The purpose is to encourage the candid participation of experts and others who may have information that would facilitate resolution of the case. . . .

SECTION 5. WAIVER AND PRECLUSION OF PRIVILEGE.

(a) A privilege under Section 4 may be waived in a record or orally during a proceeding if it is expressly waived by all parties to the mediation and:

(1) in the case of the privilege of a mediator, it is expressly waived by the mediator; and

(2) in the case of the privilege of a nonparty participant, it is expressly waived by the nonparty participant.

(b) A person that discloses or makes a representation about a mediation communication which prejudices another person in a proceeding is precluded from asserting a privilege under Section 4, but only to the extent necessary for the person prejudiced to respond to the representation or disclosure.

(c) A person that intentionally uses a mediation to plan, attempt to commit or commit a crime, or to conceal an ongoing crime or ongoing criminal activity is precluded from asserting a privilege under Section 4.

Reporter's Notes

1. Section 5(a) and (b). Waiver and preclusion.

[T]hese provisions differ from the attorney-client privilege in that the mediation privilege does not permit waiver to be implied by conduct. The rationale for requiring explicit waiver is to safeguard against the possibility of inadvertent waiver, such as through the often salutary practice of parties discussing their dispute and mediation with friends and relatives. In contrast to these settings, there is a sense of formality and awareness of legal rights in all of the proceedings to which the privilege may be waived if the waiver is oral. They generally are conducted on the record, easing the difficulties of establishing what was said.

[Requiring explicit waiver] created the anomalous situation of permitting the opportunity for one party to blurt out potentially damaging information in the midst of a trial and then use the privilege to block the other party from contesting the truth. To address this anomaly, the Drafters added Section 5(b), a preclusion provision to cover situations in which the parties do not expressly waive the privilege but engage in conduct inconsistent with the assertions of the privilege, and that cause prejudice. As under existing interpretations for other communications privileges, waiver through preclusion would not typically constitute a waiver with respect to all mediation communications, only those related in subject matter. . . .

2. Section 5(c). Preclusion for use of mediation to plan or commit crime.

. . . This Section should be read together with Section 6(a)(4), which applies to particular communications within a mediation which are used for the same purposes. The two differ on the purpose of the mediation: Section 5(c) applies when the mediation itself is used to further a crime, while Section 6(a)(4) applies to matters that are being mediated for other purposes but which include discussion of acts or statements that may be deemed criminal in nature. Under

Section 5(c), the preclusion applies to all mediation communications because the purpose of the mediation frustrates public policy. Under Section 6(a)(4), the preclusion only applies to those mediation communications that have a criminal character; the privilege may still be asserted to block the introduction of other communications made during the mediation. . . .

SECTION 6. EXCEPTIONS TO PRIVILEGE.

(a) There is no privilege under Section 4 for a mediation communication that is:

(1) in an agreement evidenced by a record signed by all parties to the agreement;

(2) available to the public under [insert statutory reference to open records act] or made during a session of a mediation which is open, or is required by law to be open, to the public;

(3) a threat or statement of a plan to inflict bodily injury or commit a crime of violence;

(4) intentionally used to plan a crime, attempt to commit or commit a crime, or to conceal an ongoing crime or ongoing criminal activity;

(5) sought or offered to prove or disprove a claim or complaint of professional misconduct or malpractice filed against a mediator;

(6) except as otherwise provided in subsection (c), sought or offered to prove or disprove a claim or complaint of professional misconduct or malpractice filed against a mediation party, nonparty participant, or representative of a party based on conduct occurring during a mediation; or

(7) sought or offered to prove or disprove abuse, neglect, abandonment, or exploitation in a proceeding in which a child or adult protective services agency is a party, unless the

[Alternative A: [State to insert, for example, child or adult protection] case is referred by a court to mediation and a public agency participates.]

[Alternative B: public agency participates in the [State to insert, for example, child or adult protection] mediation].

(b) There is no privilege under Section 4 if a court, administrative agency, or arbitrator finds, after a hearing in camera, that the party seeking discovery or the proponent of the evidence has shown that the evidence is not otherwise available, that there is a need for the evidence that substantially outweighs the interest in protecting confidentiality, and that the mediation communication is sought or offered in:

(1) a court proceeding involving a felony [or misdemeanor]; or

(2) except as otherwise provided in subsection (c), a proceeding to prove a claim to rescind or reform or a defense to avoid liability on a contract arising out of the mediation.

(c) A mediator may not be compelled to provide evidence of a mediation communication referred to in subsection (a)(6) or (b)(2).

(d) If a mediation communication is not privileged under subsection (a) or (b), only the portion of the communication necessary for the application of the exception from nondisclosure may be admitted. Admission of evidence under subsection (a) or (b) does not render the evidence, or any other mediation communication, discoverable or admissible for any other purpose.

Reporter's Notes

1. In general.

The exceptions in Section 6(a) apply regardless of the need for the evidence because society's interest in the information contained in the mediation communications may be said to categorically outweigh its interest in the confidentiality of mediation communications. In contrast, the exceptions under Section 6(b) would apply only in situations where the relative strengths of society's interest in a mediation communication and mediation participant interest in confidentiality can only be measured under the facts and circumstances of the particular case....

2. Section 6(a)(1). Record of an agreement.

... This exception is noteworthy only for what is not included: oral agreements. The disadvantage of exempting oral settlements is that nearly everything said during a mediation session could bear on either whether the parties came to an agreement or the content of the agreement. In other words, an exception for oral agreements has the potential to swallow the rule of privilege. As a result, mediation participants might be less candid, not knowing whether a controversy later would erupt over an oral agreement. Unfortunately, excluding evidence of oral settlements reached during a mediation session would operate to the disadvantage of a less legally sophisticated party who is accustomed to the enforcement of oral settlements reached in negotiations. Such a person might also mistakenly assume the admissibility of evidence of oral settlements reached in mediation as well. However, because the majority of courts and statutes limit the confidentiality exception to signed written agreements, one would expect that mediators and others will soon incorporate knowledge of a writing requirement into their practices. Despite the limitation on oral agreements, the Act leaves parties other means to preserve the agreement quickly. For example, parties can agree that the mediation has ended, state their oral agreement into the tape recorder and record their assent....

3. **Section 6(a)(2). Mediations open to the public; meetings and records made open by law.**

Section 6(a)(2) makes clear that the privileges in Section 4 do not preempt state open meetings and open records laws, thus deferring to the policies of the individual States regarding the types of meetings that will be subject to these laws. In addition, it provides an exception when the mediation is opened to the public, such as a televised mediation. . . .

5. **Section 6(a)(4). Communications used to plan or commit a crime.**

[T]his exception does not cover mediation communications constituting admissions of past crimes, or past potential crimes, which remain privileged. Thus, for example, discussions of past aggressive positions with regard to taxation or other matters of regulatory compliance in commercial mediations remain privileged against possible use in subsequent or simultaneous civil proceedings. The Drafting Committees discussed the possibility of creating an exception for the related circumstance in which a party makes an admission of past conduct that portends future bad conduct. However, they decided against such an expansion of this exception because such past conduct can already be disclosed in other important ways. The other parties can warn others, because parties are not prohibited from disclosing by the Act. . . .

7. **Section 6(a)(6). Evidence of professional misconduct or malpractice by a party or representative of a party.**

Sometimes the issue arises whether anyone may provide evidence of professional misconduct or malpractice occurring during the mediation. The failure to provide an exception for such evidence would mean that lawyers and fiduciaries could act unethically or in violation of standards without concern that evidence of the misconduct would later be admissible in a proceeding brought for recourse. This exception makes it possible to use testimony of anyone except the mediator in proceedings at which such a claim is made or defended. Because of the potential adverse impact on a mediator's appearance of impartiality, the use of mediator testimony is more guarded, and therefore protected by Section 6(c). . . . Mediators and others are not precluded by the Act from reporting misconduct to an agency or tribunal other than one that might make a ruling on the dispute being mediated, which is precluded by Section 8(a) and (b).

Appendix J   Uniform Mediation Act (2002)

8. Section 6(a)(7). Evidence of abuse or neglect.

An exception for child abuse and neglect is common in domestic mediation confidentiality statutes, and the Act reaffirms these important policy choices States have made to protect their citizens. By referring to "child and adult protective services agency," the exception broadens the coverage to include the elderly and disabled if that State has protected them by statute and has created an agency enforcement process. It should be stressed that this exception applies only to permit disclosures in public agency proceedings in which the agency is a party or nonparty participant. The exception does not apply in private actions, such as divorce, because the need for the evidence is not as great as in proceedings brought to protect against abuse and neglect so that the harm can be stopped, and is outweighed by the policy of promoting candor during mediation. For example, in a mediation between Husband and Wife who are seeking a divorce, Husband admits to sexually abusing a child. Husband's admission would not be privileged in an action brought by the public agency to protect the child, but would be privileged in the divorce hearings. The last bracketed phrases make an exception to the exception to privilege of mediation communications in certain mediations involving such public agencies. . . . These alternatives are bracketed and offered to the states as recommended model provisions because of concerns raised by some mediators of such cases that mediator testimony sometimes can be necessary and appropriate to secure the safety of a vulnerable party in a situation of abuse.

9. Section 6(b). Exceptions requiring demonstration of need.

The exceptions under this Section constitute less common fact patterns that may sometimes justify carving an exception, but only when the unique facts and circumstances of the case demonstrate that the evidence is otherwise unavailable, and the need for the evidence outweighs the policies underlying the privilege. Thus, Section 6(b) effectively places the burden on the proponent to persuade the court on these points. The evidence will not be disclosed absent a finding on these points after an in camera hearing. Further, under Section 6(d) the evidence will be admitted only for that limited purpose.

10. Section 6(b)(1). Felony [and misdemeanors].

[T]he Act affords more specialized treatment for the use of mediation communications in subsequent felony proceedings, which reflects the unique character, considerations, and concerns that attend the need for evidence in the criminal process. States may also wish to extend this specialized treatment to misdemeanors, and the Drafters offer appropriate model language for states in that event.

Existing privilege statutes are silent or split as to whether they apply only to civil proceedings, apply also to some juvenile or misdemeanor proceedings, or apply as well to all criminal proceedings. The split among the States reflects clashing policy interests. On the one hand, mediation participants operating under the benefit of a privilege might reasonably expect that statements made in mediation would not be available for use in a later felony prosecution. The candor this expectation promotes is precisely that which the mediation privilege seeks to protect. It is also the basis upon which many criminal courts throughout the country have established victim-offender mediation programs, which have enjoyed great success in misdemeanor, and, increasingly, felony cases. Public policy specifically supports the mediation of gang disputes, for example, and these programs may be less successful if the parties cannot discuss the criminal acts underlying the disputes.

On the other hand, society's need for evidence to avoid an inaccurate decision is greatest in the criminal context—both for evidence that might convict the guilty and exonerate the innocent—because the stakes of human liberty and public safety are at their zenith. For this reason, even without this exception, the courts can be expected to weigh heavily the need for the evidence in a particular case, and sometimes will rule that the defendant's constitutional rights require disclosure.

After great consideration and public comment, the Drafting Committees decided to leave the critical balancing of these competing interests to the sound discretion of the courts to determine under the facts and circumstances of each case. Critically, it is drafted in a manner to ensure the same right to evidence introduced by the prosecution, thus assuring a level playing field. In addition, it puts the parties on notice of this limitation on confidentiality.

11. Section 6(b)(2). Validity and enforceability of settlement agreement.

This exception is designed to preserve traditional contract defenses to the enforcement of the mediated settlement agreement that relate to the integrity of the mediation process, which otherwise would be unavailable if based on mediation communications. A recent Texas case provides an example. An action was brought to enforce a mediated settlement. The defendant raised the defense of duress and sought to introduce evidence that he had asked the mediator to permit him to leave because of chest pains and a history of heart trouble, and that the mediator had refused to let him leave the mediation session. *See Randle v. Mid Gulf, Inc.*, No. 14-95-01292, 1996 WL 447954 (Tex. App. 1996) (unpublished). The exception might also allow party testimony in a personal injury case that the driver denied having insurance, causing the plaintiff to rely and settle on that basis, where such a misstatement would be a basis for reforming or avoiding liability under the settlement. Under this exception the evidence will not be privileged if the weighing requirements are met. This exception differs from the exception for a record of an agreement in Section 6(a)(1) in that Section 6(a)(1) only exempts the admissibility of the record of the agreement itself, while the exception in Section 6(b)(2) is broader in that it would permit the admissibility of other mediation communications that are necessary to establish or refute a defense to the validity of a mediated settlement agreement. . . .

SECTION 7. PROHIBITED MEDIATOR REPORTS.

(a) Except as required in subsection (b), a mediator may not make a report, assessment, evaluation, recommendation, finding, or other communication regarding a mediation to a court, administrative agency, or other authority that may make a ruling on the dispute that is the subject of the mediation.

(b) A mediator may disclose:

(1) whether the mediation occurred or has terminated, whether a settlement was reached, and attendance;

(2) a mediation communication as permitted under Section 6; or

(3) a mediation communication evidencing abuse, neglect, abandonment, or exploitation of an individual to a public agency responsible for protecting individuals against such mistreatment.

(c) A communication made in violation of subsection (a) may not be considered by a court, administrative agency, or arbitrator.

Reporter's Notes

. . . In contrast to the privilege, which gives a right to refuse to provide evidence in a subsequent legal proceeding, this Section creates a prohibition against disclosure. . . .The purpose of this Section is consistent with the conclusions of seminal reports in the mediation field [that] condemn the use of such reports as permitting coercion by the mediator and destroying confidence in the neutrality of the mediator and in the mediation process.

Importantly, the prohibition is limited to reports or other listed communications to those who may rule on the dispute being mediated. While the mediators are thus constrained in terms of reports to courts and others that may make rulings on the case, they are not prohibited from reporting threatened harm to appropriate authorities, for example, if learned during a mediation to settle a civil dispute. In this regard, Section 7(b)(3) responds to public concerns about clarity and makes explicit what is otherwise implied in the Act, that mediators are not constrained by this Section in their ability to disclose threats to the safety and well being of vulnerable parties to appropriate public authorities, and is consistent with the exception for disclosure in proceedings in Section 6(a)(7). Similarly, while the provision prohibits mediators from making these reports, it does not constrain the parties.

The communications by the mediator to the court or other authority are broadly defined. The provisions would not permit a mediator to communicate, for example, on whether a particular party engaged in "good faith" negotiation, or to state whether a party had been "the problem" in reaching a settlement. Section 7(b)(1), however, does permit disclosure of particular facts, including attendance and whether a settlement was reached. For example, a mediator may report that one party did not attend and another attended only for the first five minutes. States with "good faith" mediation laws or court rules may want to consider the interplay between such laws and this Section of the Act.

SECTION 8. CONFIDENTIALITY.

Unless subject to the [insert statutory references to open meetings act and open records act], mediation communications are confidential to the extent agreed by the parties or provided by other law or rule of this State.

Reporter's Notes

This Section restates the general rule in the states regarding the confidentiality of mediation communications outside the context of proceedings. Typically, confidentiality agreements are enforceable against a signatory under state contract law, through damages and sometimes specific enforcement. . . .

Early drafts were criticized by some in the mediation community for failing to impose an affirmative duty on mediation participants not to disclose mediation communications to third persons outside of the context of the proceedings at which the Section 4 privilege applies. In several subsequent drafts, the Drafters attempted to establish a rule that would prohibit such disclosures, but found it impracticable to do so without imposing a severe risk of civil liability on the many unknowing mediation participants who might discuss their mediations with friends and family members, for example, for any number of salutary reasons. In addition, the Drafters were deeply concerned about their capacity to develop a truly comprehensive list of legitimate and appropriate exceptions — such as for the education and training of mediators, for the monitoring evaluation and improvement of court-related mediation programs, and for the reporting of threats to police and abuse to public agencies—as each draft drew forth more calls for legitimate and appropriate exceptions. Similarly, efforts to create a simpler rule with fewer exceptions but with greater judicial discretion to act as appropriate on a case-by-case basis to prevent "manifest injustice" also met severe resistance from many different sectors of the mediation community, as well as a number of state bar ADR committees. Finally, recognizing the important role of non-lawyer mediators and the many people who participate in mediations without counsel or knowledge of the law, the Drafters were concerned about the intelligibility and accessibility of the provisions. In the end, the Drafters ultimately chose to draw a clear line, and to follow the general practice in the states of leaving the disclosure of mediation communications outside of proceedings to the good judgment of the parties to determine in light of the unique characteristics and circumstances of their dispute. . . .

SECTION 9. MEDIATOR'S DISCLOSURE OF CONFLICTS OF INTEREST; BACKGROUND.

(a) Before accepting a mediation, an individual who is requested to serve as a mediator shall:

(1) make an inquiry that is reasonable under the circumstances to determine whether there are any known facts that a reasonable individual would consider likely to affect the impartiality of the mediator, including a financial or personal interest in the outcome of the mediation and an existing or past relationship with a mediation party or foreseeable participant in the mediation; and

(2) disclose any such known fact to the mediation parties as soon as is practical before accepting a mediation.

(b) If a mediator learns any fact described in subsection (a)(1) after accepting a mediation, the mediator shall disclose it as soon as is practicable.

(c) At the request of a mediation party, an individual who is requested to serve as a mediator shall disclose the mediator's qualifications to mediate a dispute.

(d) A person that violates subsection [(a) or (b)][(a), (b), or (g)] is precluded by the violation from asserting a privilege under Section 4.

(e) Subsections (a), (b), [and] (c), [and] [(g)] do not apply to an individual acting as a judge.

(f) This [Act] does not require that a mediator have a special qualification by background or profession.

[(g) A mediator must be impartial, unless after disclosure of the facts required in subsections (a) and (b) to be disclosed, the parties agree otherwise.]

Reporter's Notes

> 1. *Sections 9(a) and 9(b). Disclosure of mediator's conflicts of interest.* ...
>
> b. Reasonable duty of inquiry
> ... The reasonable inquiry ... depends on the circumstances. For example, if a small claims court refers parties to a mediator who has a volunteer attorney standing in court, the parties would not expect that mediator to check on conflicts with all lawyers in the mediator's firm in the five minutes between referral and mediation. Presumably, only conflicts known by the mediator would affect that mediation in any event.
>
> 2. *Section 9(c) and (f). Disclosure of mediator's qualifications.*

It must be stressed that the Act does not establish mediator qualifications. No consensus has emerged in the law, research, or commentary as to those mediator qualifications that will best produce effectiveness or fairness. As clarified by Section 9(f), mediators need not be lawyers. In fact, the American Bar Association Section on Dispute Resolution has issued a statement that "dispute resolution programs should permit all individuals who have appropriate training and qualifications to serve as neutrals, regardless of whether they are lawyers." ABA Section of Dispute Resolution Council Res., April 28, 1999.

At the same time, the law and commentary recognize that the quality of the mediator is important and that the courts and public agencies referring cases to mediation have a heightened responsibility to assure it. The decision of the Drafting Committees against prescribing qualifications should not be interpreted as a disregard for the importance of qualifications. Rather, respecting the unique characteristics that may qualify a particular mediator for a particular mediation, the silence of the Act reflects the difficulty of addressing the topic in a uniform statute that applies to mediation in a variety of contexts. Qualifications may be important, but they need not be uniform. It is not the intent of the Act to preclude a statute, court or administrative agency rule, arbitrator or contract between the parties from requiring that a mediator have a particular background or profession; those decisions are best made by individual states, courts, governmental entities, and parties.

> 5. *[Section 9(g). Mediator impartiality.]*

This provision is a bracketed to signal that it is suggested as a model provision and need not be part of a Uniform Act. ... While few would argue that it is almost always best for mediators to be impartial as a matter of practice, including such a requirement into a uniform law drew considerable controversy. Some mediators, reflecting a deeply and sincerely felt value within the mediation community that a mediator not be predisposed to favor or disfavor parties in dispute, persistently urged the Drafters to enshrine this value in the Act; for these, the failure to include the notion of impartiality in the Act would be a distortion of the mediation process. Other mediators, service providers, judges, mediation scholars, however, urged the Drafters not to include the term "impartiality" for a variety of reasons. At least three are worth stressing. One pressing concern was that including such a statutory requirement would subject mediators to an unwarranted exposure to civil lawsuits by disgruntled parties. In this regard, mediators with a more evaluative style expressed concerns that the common practice of so-called "reality checking" would be used as a basis for such actions against the mediator. A second major concern was over the workability of such a statutory requirement. Scholarly research in cognitive psychology has confirmed many hidden but common biases that affect judgment, such as attributional distortions of judgment and inclinations that are the product of social learning and professional culturation. Similarly, mediators in certain contexts sometimes have an ethical or felt duty to advocate on behalf of a party, such as long-term care ombuds in the health care context. Third, some parties seek to use a mediator who has a duty to be partial in some respects—such as a domestic mediator who is charged by law to protect the interests of the children. It has been argued that such mediations should still be privileged. . . .

SECTION 10. PARTICIPATION IN MEDIATION.

An attorney or other individual designated by a party may accompany the party to and participate in a mediation. A waiver of participation given before the mediation may be rescinded.

Reporter's Notes

The fairness of mediation is premised upon the informed consent of the parties to any agreement reached. Some statutes permit the mediator to exclude lawyers from mediation, resting fairness guarantees on the lawyer's later review of the draft settlement agreement. At least one bar authority has expressed doubts about the ability of a lawyer to review an agreement effectively when that lawyer did not participate in the give and take of negotiation. Boston Bar Ass'n, Op. 78-1 (1979). . . . Some parties may prefer not to bring counsel. However, because of the capacity of attorneys to help mitigate power imbalances, and in the absence of other procedural protections for less powerful parties, the Drafting Committees elected to let the parties, not the mediator, decide. Also, their agreement to exclude counsel should be made after the dispute arises, so that they can weigh the importance in the context of the stakes involved. . . .

As a practical matter, this provision has application only when the parties are compelled to participate in the mediation by contract, law, or order from a court or agency. In other instances, any party or mediator unhappy with the decision of a party to be accompanied by an individual can simply leave the mediation. In some instances, a party may seek to bring an individual whose presence will interfere with effective discussion. In divorce mediation, for example, a new friend of one of the parties may spark new arguments. In these instances, the mediator can make that observation to the parties and, if the mediation flounders because of the presence of the nonparty, the parties or the mediator can terminate the mediation. The pre-mediation waiver of this right of accompaniment can be rescinded, because the party may not have understood the implication at that point in the process. However, this provision can be waived once the mediation begins.

SECTION 11. RELATION TO ELECTRONIC SIGNATURES IN GLOBAL AND NATIONAL COMMERCE ACT.

This [Act] modifies, limits, or supersedes the federal Electronic Signatures in Global and National Commerce Act, 15 U.S.C. Section 7001 et seq., but this [Act] does not modify, limit, or supersede Section 101(c) of that Act or authorize electronic delivery of any of the notices described in Section 103(b) of that Act.

SECTION 12. UNIFORMITY OF APPLICATION AND CONSTRUCTION.

In applying and construing this [Act], consideration should be given to the need to promote uniformity of the law with respect to its subject matter among States that enact it.

SECTION 13. SEVERABILITY CLAUSE.

If any provision of this [Act] or its application to any person or circumstance is held invalid, the invalidity does not affect other provisions or applications of this [Act] which can be given effect without the invalid provision or application, and to this end the provisions of this [Act] are severable.

SECTION 14. EFFECTIVE DATE.

This [Act] takes effect ....

SECTION 15. REPEALS.

The following acts and parts of acts are hereby repealed:
(1)
(2)
(3)

SECTION 16. APPLICATION TO EXISTING AGREEMENTS OR REFERRALS.

(a) This [Act] governs a mediation pursuant to a referral or an agreement to mediate made on or after [the effective date of this [Act]].

(b) On or after [a delayed date], this [Act] governs an agreement to mediate whenever made.